A Purpose to RISE

A Purpose to Rise
A Parable of Determination & Success

Gary and Susan Harper

All Rights Reserved. No portion of this book may be reproduced, stored in a retrieval system, or transmitted in any form or by any means – electronic, mechanical, photocopy, recording, scanning, or other – except for brief quotations in critical reviews or articles without the prior permission of the author.

Published by Game Changer Publishing

Paperback ISBN: 978-1-962656-31-3
Hardcover ISBN: 978-1-962656-32-0
Digital: ISBN: 978-1-962656-33-7

www.GameChangerPublishing.com

DEDICATION

In loving memory of Ada and Gary Harper, Sr.
Though physically absent, your presence lives on within me. This book is a tribute to the extraordinary parents you were and the profound impact you had on my life. Your love, wisdom, and unwavering support continue to guide me even in your absence.

Mom, your nurturing soul and boundless affection shaped the person I have become. Your selflessness and sacrifices taught me the true meaning of love and resilience. I carry your spirit within me as I embark on this literary journey. I will KEEP GOING!

Dad, your strength, guidance, and unwavering belief in my abilities continue to inspire me every day. Your words of wisdom and your unwavering presence in my life have fueled my determination to pursue my dreams relentlessly. I honor you in every word written within these pages.

I am also grateful for the foundation of faith in God that you instilled within me. Our shared belief in His guidance and grace has been instrumental in helping me overcome challenges and achieve my goals. Through the highs and lows of this creative endeavor, I have found solace and strength in knowing that God is with me every step of the way.

Though I cannot share the joy of this accomplishment with you in person, I know that you are watching from above, cheering me on with pride. This book stands as a testament to the love, values, and faith in

God that you instilled in me, and it is dedicated to preserving your memory and the profound impact you had on my life.

Thank you for being the greatest parents a child could ever ask for. Though our time together was cut short, your legacy lives on through the pages of this book, the memories we shared, and the faith that continues to guide me.

With eternal love and gratitude,
Gary Harper

But First

Thank you so much for buying and reading our book.
We are so grateful!

Please scan this QR code to take a free online business assessment to further your understanding of where you are struggling and direct you to success.

This will help your business RISE to 100%!

You can take our free online business assessment

by scanning the QR code below:

A Purpose to RISE

A Parable of Determination & Success

Gary and Susan Harper

www.GameChangerPublishing.com

Table of Contents

Introduction 1

Chapter 1 – The Problem 3

Chapter 2 – The Brother 7

Chapter 3 – The Sister 11

Chapter 4 – The Passion 19

Chapter 5 – The Book Signing 27

Chapter 6 – The Failure 31

Chapter 7 – The Tenant 37

Chapter 8 – The Investor 41

Chapter 9 – The Meltdown 47

Chapter 10 – The Coach 53

Chapter 11 – The Assessment 59

Chapter 12 – The Accountability 65

Chapter 13 – The Resource Plan 73

Chapter 14 – The Resource Wrap-Up 83

Chapter 15 – The Weekly Meeting 87

Chapter 16 – The Leadership Assessment 93

Chapter 17 – The Leadership Audit 103

Chapter 18 – The Core Values 109

Chapter 19 – The Company's Purpose 123

Chapter 20 – The Company's Culture 127

Chapter 21 – Systems Day 133

Chapter 22 – The Meetings 139

Chapter 23 – The KPIs 147

Chapter 24 – The Culture Meeting 155

Chapter 25 – The Tactical Meeting 165

Chapter 26 – The Procedures 175

Chapter 27 – Quarterly Day 181

Chapter 28 – The Glue 191

Chapter 29 – The FOCUS 195

Chapter 30 – The Broken Dream 205

Chapter 31 – Engagement Day 213

Chapter 32 – The New Foundation 219

Chapter 33 – The End 227

Introduction

Matt Wellington yearns for a freedom that his current job and boss don't permit. He plans to start a real estate company with his brother in their hometown of Grant City. However, Matt's brother, Allan, has a slight adjustment to the plan. Despite Matt's resistance, Allan insists on including their younger sister, Charlotte, in the company.

Two years after starting, their money dries up, and pressure mounts. Matt finds himself headed off to unclog toilets in rentals and patch drywall in flips because no one wants to work without pay.

When tension between the siblings becomes combustible, Matt hires Reggie Singer, an owner and coach at RISE. Over four different meetings spanning a year, Reggie guides the Wellington siblings through their personal conflicts and business plateaus, focusing on resources, inspiration, systems, and engagement.

As Matt's initial (and unrealistic) vision for his business fades under Reggie Singer's coaching, he refines the business's objectives. This change causes Allan to quit, revealing his predisposition to dismiss Charlotte as a viable option to run the business.

In the end, Reggie's coaching results in Allan becoming an investor/owner, Matt assuming the role of CEO/owner, and Charlotte finding the freedom she sought by coaching other businesses through the RISE program.

CHAPTER 1

The Problem

January mornings are cold, especially when you live in Chicago. On a normal morning, Matt might stay in bed a little longer and work from home so he could skip defrosting his car. Today was not a normal day.

In two hours, Matt had to be at O'Hare to pick up his boss, who was inbound on an early-bird flight. Matt checked his phone. The flight was in the air and due to arrive a few minutes early.

He could not be late. The moment Kevin, the VP of Operations, stepped out of that airport, they would hurry off to the office and only have a few hours to prepare for a client meeting.

For the third time, Matt dragged hangers across the closet's rod to get a good look at each suit he owned. This was a big decision. He wasn't just a chauffeur today. Matt was presenting to the client.

Would he say the right things? Would he wear the right clothes? Would anyone notice the rings under his eyes because he hadn't slept, stressing and obsessing over the opportunity?

He went with the fourth suit he tried on, the beige one. He ironed his black shirt, slipped it on, and knotted a new tie that melded the beige and black. It looked good. It fit his age. At 27, he felt professional but modern.

He pulled up to the curb at O'Hare and hopped out of his car to care for his boss' bags.

"Nice flight, Kevin?" Matt extended his hand to his boss.

Kevin grimaced and didn't shake hands. "Why are you wearing a black shirt? That's not professional, especially for this client!"

"Don't worry. They will be so focused on my presentation that they won't notice my clothes. It's that good." Matt's smile covered the sinking feeling in his heart.

"Can we hurry this along? The presentation starts in three hours."

They arrived at the office. After three intense weeks of preparation, it was time to preview the presentation for Kevin.

"This better be good, Matt. There is no room for error." Kevin took the only water bottle on the conference table and twisted it open.

Matt took a few deep breaths. He expected his hard work to be criticized. Kevin had an abrasive and controlling leadership style. Matt never knew where Kevin stood. He never knew where Kevin was leaning. He wanted stable direction, but every project seemed like it was at the mercy of Kevin's bad mood.

Matt straightened his shoulders, optimistic that "Kevin the Dictator" would see the glory and genius of the proposal.

Matt launched into his presentation, casting a slideshow on the conference room monitor. "This is my plan for renewing the contracts." As he explained the plan, he knew better than to gauge the reception by looking at Kevin's face. Matt advanced to the next slide. "Here are the cost savings I identified in equipment and labor."

Kevin scrutinized the numbers and dismissively waved his hand at the slides. "No! Seriously, Matt! Look at how much less we'd be billing them under this new plan!"

"Kevin," Matt used his pleading voice, "lowering the monthly billable is vital. You know the economy. It's more competitive. We must deliver more value with cost reductions. They told you they will renew if the price is right."

Kevin's sigh was loud. He held up his hand to silence Matt. "We need to cut this short. I'm changing the proposal. Increase the price to be in line with the current revenue run rate. That's final."

"Why do we have to cut this short?" Matt looked at the digital clock on the wall. "We still have time."

Kevin rose from his seat and raised his nose even higher. "No. We don't. We need to cut this short because you need to change your black shirt!"

Matt retreated to his office and snapped a pencil in two. He had spent time with this client. He knew what they wanted. He knew that Kevin wasn't offering it.

On top of that, there was no way he was changing his shirt.

Two hours later, Matt and Kevin walked into the client's office to set up and prepare for the presentation. The client's leadership team entered the room. Everyone greeted each other. Though he had left Matt hanging at the airport curb, Kevin shook the hand of every client rep. His plastered smile was as fake as the alleged savings Kevin added to the proposal.

After the introductions, Matt presented his title slide. "Thanks for allowing us to present a renewal proposal. We hope that after fifteen years of uninterrupted partnership, we can continue to do business."

The client's VP spoke up. "I hope it's good and delivers us some kind of cost savings. You are going to need it to compete with the other proposals."

Matt hoped that the crestfallen feeling in his heart hadn't leaked onto his face. He smiled and nodded and went to the second slide.

At the end of his presentation, Matt said, "Thank you for allowing us to present our proposal. Are there any questions?"

Several hands shot up. Matt called on a woman. "How does this save us money over our current contract?"

Matt froze. He wanted to look at Kevin and say, "See? I told you so!" He wanted to say to the client, "My boss is a neanderthal when it comes to listening to anyone's needs and opinions. He just grunts."

Kevin rose from his seat and offered a long-winded explanation of the proposal's increased value, which justified the same cost.

No one sitting at the table could hide the disappointment on their faces. Matt looked at the client contact, hoping his face conveyed a non-verbal apology.

The client contact said, "Well…there is a lot to think about here; we will give you a call."

Matt's heart sank. The contact had told him that they would renew on the spot if the price was right. Failure washed over him. If Kevin had only listened to him, this meeting would have ended differently.

The client's team rushed out of the room, leaving Matt and Kevin alone with the impending failure.

Kevin started packing his bag. "I think it went well."

"I'm not so sure." Matt weighed his next words. He had to respect his boss, so he stuffed his anger. "How do you think I did with the presentation?"

"I don't know. I was distracted by the ugly black shirt I told you to change."

CHAPTER 2

The Brother

After the long ride home through rush hour traffic, the rest of the night promised to be longer. Matt couldn't sleep as he thought about what could have been. He lay on his bed and stared at the ceiling. That's exactly what Kevin was: a ceiling. Kevin was something hovering over his head, stunting his growth and interfering with Matt's rise to success.

Matt's cell phone buzzed with a text from his brother, Allan.

"How did it go today?"

Matt began typing a message, deleted it, and called his brother.

"It was that bad that you had to call?" Allan asked.

"Sometimes in this job with my boss, I feel like I'm crammed into a clown car with my face pressed up against the ceiling."

"That's why I never chased the city life and stayed home," Allan said.

Matt picked up the picture of him and Allan and James Burks from Matt's senior year of high school. "And there are reasons I didn't stay home."

"You're just a short drive away if you and Jean want to visit this weekend now that the presentation is over."

"No thanks. Jean went to see her sister. She didn't want to be around me as I stressed out about the proposal. She's coming back Monday."

"So what can I do for you?"

"Nothing."

"Then why did you call?"

"Because you're my little brother, who is bigger than me. You're stable. Chasing my dreams gets discouraging sometimes, and it's good for me to hear your voice."

"I love you, too, Matt!"

"Thanks, Allan."

"There's something else. I know you. There's something else."

Matt sighed. "Do you ever think about doing something different?"

"No. I like my wife. I like my two kids. I like my job. I like where I live. I've done a good job investing my inheritance money. You thinking about making a change?"

"A couple of Saturdays ago, right after New Year's, I saw this guy come out of a restaurant with a steaming take-out box, and he gave it to a homeless man who begs near the diner around the corner."

"You want to open a homeless shelter? Doesn't sound like you'd love that."

"No, Allan. The homeless guy opens the Styrofoam container, and it has a burger and fries. You should have seen the happiness."

"I'm sure a homeless guy would be happy to get a fresh burger and fries."

"No. I'm talking about the joy on the face of the guy who gave it to him. I don't remember the last time I had that pure of a smile. This guy's name is Juan. He sees me looking at them, and do you know what he asks me?"

"He asked you, 'What are you looking at, punk?'"

"No. Some people in Chicago are nice. He asked me, 'Do you need a burger?' and he was just happy. So we go inside the diner and just talk. He's a real estate developer, Juan Perez. He purchased and was renovating apartment buildings near his apartment. He talked about the freedom of being his own boss, the development of employees, and the personal satisfaction of improving Chicago. He didn't sugarcoat anything. He talked about the investment, the hours, the sweat, the grind."

"Sounds harder than what you are doing now."

"None of those things deterred me. He just had this freedom, and I want that freedom."

"What do you know about real estate?"

"Today? Nothing."

"If anyone could learn something new, it would be you. Hey, if it would get you back home, come fix up Grant City like he's fixing up Chicago." Allan laughed.

"Maybe I will."

"That would be the day, Matthew. You ran from here as soon as you could. You didn't even go to your ten-year reunion this past fall."

Matt looked at the basketball picture again. Then he looked at the picture of his parents. "Maybe there were things to run from, Allan."

"Maybe. But don't run from your sister. We haven't seen you since her high school graduation."

"I think you've reminded me of that a half dozen times lately."

"Do you even talk to Charlotte?"

"We just don't have much in common. She's so spacey, jumping from art project to music project to design project to fashion project."

"She's a sophomore now."

"I know. I see her on social media. I keep up. Just not in a personal way. Are you sure there's room in your guest room if I visit, or are her canvases in there?"

"Ha! Like you'll visit. Well, let me know if I can help you in your search for freedom. I'm here for you, Matt."

"Thanks, Allan. I love you. Bye."

"Love you, too."

Matt ended the call, brushed his teeth, and lay in his bed.

His mind immediately went to the failed proposal.

What if Kevin had been more of a leader than a dictator? What if Kevin had tried to help me grow instead of tying me down?

Matt burned with a desire to run his own company. He sat up in bed, turned on his lamp, and grabbed a journal. He listed what he thought it would take to be a leader running his own company.

He wanted his own real estate business.

That's right! No more selling widgets and servicing gizmos. Today was the final straw. Someday, his own real estate investing business would thrive because he would be a leader who empowered his people.

Matt doodled Kevin's name in large block letters that conveyed the rage he wanted to aim at his boss. Matt then furiously slashed Xs through the name. Then he took a deep breath…and repeatedly stabbed "Kevin" with his pen.

Kevin is ruining my career.

He calmed once again and scratched three words into his journal: "Leadership versus Dictatorship." Only one was truly scalable. Under the dictatorship, he would be stuck and not growing. Matt wanted out. He wanted out of Kevin's grasp. He wanted out of the bondage of being an employee. He wanted to rise.

CHAPTER 3

The Sister

Matt clasped his hands in a begging posture. "Allan, remember that you said that I should let you know if you could help me in my search for freedom—"

"How many years ago was that?"

"Five."

Allan dropped his spoon in his cup, splattering coffee on the diner table. "Five years? Sounds like that coupon expired. This is a lot more than an inspirational speech you are asking for."

"I will move back here. This business will make a difference in Grant City. If you invest, I can get this off the ground. You know how Dad loved those neighborhoods where he grew up? Don't you remember how sometimes, after church, we would sit in the back of that way-too-old wood-paneled station wagon?"

"Yes. Back before seat belt safety existed." Allan dabbed at each spot of coffee on the diner table.

"Right! And he would show us where Grandpa raised him and where Grandma would spank him. Where he met mom—"

"—the day he was riding his bike to return the milk bottles." With his long arm span, Allan reached across and absorbed Matt's coffee drips on the table. "I know all the stories."

"It's just $250,000 to get started. You'll be my COO and CFO until we can hire a COO. I'm the visionary. You're the integrator."

"That's a lot of money, Matt."

"You have a lot of money, Allan."

"It's not like I'm retired. Besides, what exactly are your real estate credentials, Matthew Harris Wellington?" Allan narrowed his gaze.

"I'm being mentored by—"

"Hang on! I got a text from Lisa. Got to answer it. The wife beckons."

Matt huffed as Allan swiped on his phone.

Allan turned the phone around. "Look at the picture of little Theodore. Lisa bought him and Harriet coordinating outfits for the Grant City Fourth of July Parade. I'll be 32 for 32 in making the parade. Never missed a year. You going to be in town this year for it?"

"I will be at the parade if I raise all my money and can quit my job in Chicago and start our business." Matt emphasized "our" and pointed back and forth between him and Allan.

"Oh, yes. You were telling me your credentials."

"I have been mentored by—"

"Juan Perez, I know. I vetted him on Facebook. And YouTube. And Instagram. And TikTok."

"LinkedIn?"

"Yes. I'm thorough. He checks out. Seems legit."

"He is legit!"

"But what does he know about real estate in Grant City, Indiana? It's not the same market as the west side of Chicago."

"But we know this city, Allan. You love this city. You know those old neighborhoods. Houses are crumbling. Some people live in squalor. I drove by the old movie theater." Matt's voice trailed off. He composed himself before saying, "We are going to turn it around and get the key to the city."

Allan's mouth twisted, but no words came out.

"You can tell me, Allan. I'm your brother. We can't do this unless you buy in. I'm not just talking about your money. I'm talking about buying in with your heart."

"If Matt's talking about people's hearts, he is trying to pull something over on you." Charlotte, their sister and waitress, pulled up to the table. "What are you ordering?"

Matt facetiously smiled. "I'll have the turkey club."

Charlotte tapped her pen on her pad. "No. I mean, 'What are you ordering Allan to do?' Big brothers are bossy."

Allan pointed at Charlotte and pumped his fist. "I wish I had your spunk when talking to him."

"Why is everyone ganging up on me?" Matt threw his hands in the air.

Charlotte sat down on Matt's side of the booth and pushed him over with her hips. She laid her head on his shoulder. "We love you, Matthew. You just always have been a little too harsh in wanting your way. You know, sometimes we saw that growing up." She giggled.

Matt shrugged her off his shoulder.

Matt locked eyes with his brother. "Allan?"

Allan's eyes narrowed. "Matt. I'm a numbers guy...."

"Yes. That's why I need you!" Matt slapped the table.

"Let him finish his thought!" Charlotte said.

"Don't you have other customers to wait on?" Matt pushed back with his hips, but Charlotte wouldn't budge. "You been putting on weight?"

"You've just grown weak in your years away from Grant City."

Allan reached across the table and squeezed Charlotte's hand. "Thank you, Char. Matt, I'm a numbers guy. You're a words guy. You're a great guy. When you're going good, you are looking out for the little guy, a defender. I see why you want to do this for yourself, of course, but also for Grant City. I love how you want to call the business New Grant City

Properties. I even want to see the city's improvements. I love this city, too. I just don't know if I'm good for you."

Matt's eyebrows shot up as he sat back in the booth. "What do you mean? You're perfect."

"I mean that if you're going bad and going wrong, you really become you."

"What does that mean?"

"Let me explain." Charlotte slid her hand across the table. "Sometimes you're a steamroller and obsessed with getting your way—"

"And winning! You always want to win," Allan added.

"Yes," Charlotte fist-bumped Allan. "But when you are a defender, you are obsessed with other people winning."

Allan said, "When you are a steamroller, Matt, then I'm not the person who is going to oppose you and stop you. And we'll both be ruined."

Matt pursed his lips and looked to the ceiling. "You don't understand. I will be that defender guy. I'm trying to raise you up right now, Allan. You are a genius with money. That's why you have so much liquid cash right now."

"You're asking for my life, too. You're asking me to put my family to the side."

"You and me are family!"

"I mean the time it's going to take away from Lisa and Theodore and Harriet."

"I can't lie. It's going to be a grind for a while. This has the potential to make tens of thousands of dollars from each deal."

"So, it's the money?" Allan scrutinized his brother.

"Allan, you're a wiz as an investor, and you still work a 9-to-5 job."

"I like what I do. It's comfortable. And as you may have noticed...I'm not the one asking for money."

"See! You can say things like that and stand up to me."

Allan shook his head. "I can't. Not every day, if necessary. I'm out—"

"Come on, Allan!"

"Maybe. If...."

"If what?"

Allan's eyes shifted to Charlotte.

The implication dawned on Matt. "No." He shifted away from Charlotte and closer to the wall. "You want us to take on Charlotte. Charlotte?"

"Yes."

Matt looked at his sister. "You know I love you, but you've been working on your interior design degree for two years too long, and you're not even a senior." He looked to Allan. "What would she even do?"

Charlotte leaned over, kissed Matt on the cheek, and rose from the table. "I'll come back for your order. I'm going to check on my customers."

Allan waited until she walked away. "She has a minor in business."

"She's working towards that minor. She hasn't finished any degree."

"My two girls needed Easter dresses. She looked at Lisa's easter dress—looked at it and didn't even snap a picture—and in 48 hours, made a unique little girl's dress for Harriet that matched Lisa's. She sees things. She sees things come together."

"In fabric and paint and wallpaper and furniture. She's not decorating the office for us. What do you see her doing?"

"COO."

"What? Allan, I'm the visionary, and I can't picture this."

"You're stuck on her being your little sister. She was 10 when you went to college. You've barely known her for the past fourteen years. You've been in your fraternities and internships and chasing the big-city, big-business life in Chicago instead of being around here in Grant City. You haven't seen her grow up."

"Is taking six years to finish less than three years of college the mark of a grown up? Come on, Allan. Me and you. We've always known what we've wanted from the time we were kids, and we went for it."

"Did you know, Matt? Then why are you changing what you are doing now?"

Matt sighed. "Touché. But you know the answer, Allan. We want to rise above what boys dreamed of. We didn't know the ceilings that would keep us from rising. My ceiling was bad bosses. Your ceiling is the lack of confidence in yourself. I'm trying to change that for us."

"Well, while you were discovering that, Charlotte was discovering who she was. She's sharp, Matt. She's not thirteen."

Charlotte came back over. "Know what you want yet?"

Matt smirked. "Like we've had time to look at the menu. Allan's crazy, isn't he? You wouldn't even want to be part of it."

"I would," Charlotte beamed.

"It was actually her idea," Allan added.

Matt slumped in the booth. "Talking behind my back? I feel betrayed."

Allan motioned to Charlotte. "Tell him about your ideas for a logo and branding."

Matt perked up. "What is it?"

She sat back down. "Tell me yours first."

"Okay. I like the name New Grant City. It sounds big. It sounds like we are improving Grant City. It speaks to renovating what we have. I want the logo to be an arch like St. Louis. Or a giant gate."

Charlotte nodded and set to work on a simple logo. She drew two converging lines with a dotted line in the middle and a silhouette of three skyscrapers on the horizon. Then, she drew a circle around it.

"It's a road." Matt motioned with his hands, waiting for more. "Buildings. No gate? No arch?"

Charlotte rolled her eyes. "St. Louis is two states away."

"A road? But we're not an asphalt company."

"You want a gate, and we're not a fence company."

Allan laughed. "Good one, Char!"

Charlotte looked up from her drawing. "We're New Grant City. We're taking you down new roads. There are no buildings this tall around here. The logo shows that we are future thinking in our dreams and visions."

"So?" Allan opened his arms wide.

Matt bit his lip as he thought. "It's actually not a bad idea."

"It's a good idea!" Charlotte drew a check mark next to her logo.

Matt shook his head. "I don't know."

Allan said, "Look, Matt. I'll put it on the bottom shelf. I won't give you $250,000. But I believe so much in Charlotte AND you that if you take her on, I'll give you $500,000 to start."

Matt's head shot back like he had been punched by a boxer. "What did you say?"

"Half a million. Lisa and I have been talking about it. We believe in Charlotte. And in you. And in the cause."

Matt imagined going into work on Monday and quitting. Kevin would rave and turn bright red, the vein in his neck bulging like it was a pimple about to pop.

Matt and Allan stood and embraced. Matt fought back tears. "This is like one of the top five times I've felt close to you. This will be worth the investment."

"Can I get in on this?" Charlotte nuzzled her way into the hug.

"Sure," Matt said. "Now that you're part of the team."

CHAPTER 4

The Passion

The start-up money was precious, but Matt could not pass up this mastermind in Orlando. Allan didn't seem to want to go anyway. It was too social for him. He'd have to meet people, network, and make small talk.

Charlotte had asked to come so she could mingle like a social butterfly. Her sales pitch for attending was that it would be a week with her brother, catching up after all these years. To Matt, that wasn't worth a $3,000 ticket plus travel expenses. He needed the start-up money, but he really wanted to hear the inspiration of Reggie Singer. Maybe even get to meet him.

Matt arrived at Reggie's talk in the conference room an hour early, finding a seat dead center on the first row. He clutched his copy of Reggie's book *RISE: Mending and Ascending* with the small-font subtitle that read, "Fixing your Business and Rising to Success."

Matt turned over the book and stared at Reggie's picture on the back. Matt had watched all of Reggie's social media videos. He had read this book twice and even highlighted it.

"Do you know what I think every time I see that picture?" The floppy-haired blond man plopped down two seats from Matt. His backward lanyard hid his name.

"Success. I think about success every time I see it. My area isn't quite as urban as his, but I feel like Reggie and I have the same heart."

"Wow! You're an idealist. I see that picture and think that he's trying to look like Kanye West."

"The rapper."

"Yep."

"You like rap."

"Negative." The man's surfer accent emerged as he spoke.

"You like Reggie?

"I'm apathetic. I'm in media. I just report on what's going on in the REI world for my podcast." He handed Matt a business card for www.reiworldmedia.rei. "I'm based out of SoCal."

"Thanks...." Matt scanned the card for his name. "...Slater."

"Be sure to give me five stars on your podcast app of choice." He winked at me. "Even a good review." He got up and walked away.

Nearly an hour later, Reggie Singer walked up to the backdrop at the front of the conference room. He wore shades and a bomber-style leather jacket that was fitted instead of baggy. The crowd lit up and got loud, like they were ready to cheer for their team. Matt's heart lifted. On the screen behind Reggie, a graphic emerged of the two-by-two diamond grid with the four RISE quadrants in each quarter: Resources, Inspiration, Systems, and Engagement.

Reggie lifted the mic. "I'm Reggie Singer. Yes. My Mom named me after Mr. October. She always told me that the one child she knew was going to be a home run."

The audience laughed. Except Slater. He had sat at the end of the row. Matt wondered if he knew anything about baseball. Slater didn't even smile. His face looked pained as he typed on his laptop.

Reggie removed his shades and left them on the podium. "I am a developer and partner of the RISE business framework as well as an REI investor in the New York City tri-state area. I started and sold an REI business, and I found that I love being a passive financial investor while I personally invest wisdom and value in companies like yours. Today, I want to fire up your engines because some of you have come here today with a new business venture in mind. Some of you have come here today seeking inspiration because your business needs a boost, maybe a kick in the butt. If you are going to do it...." He paused and leaned towards the audience. His gold chains jingled like wind chimes in an invigorating spring breeze. "...do you even have the passion for what you do?"

He let the question settle onto the audience. The crowd was silent except for the shifting of chairs beneath the weight of the question. Matt knew those chair shifters didn't have passion. But he did. He leaned forward.

"I'm just going to warn you now." Reggie stepped towards the audience and spoke in an exaggerated whisper. "I'm going to say some things that might hurt you." He grinned, showing off milk-white teeth. "I call those my Reggie Singer Stingers."

The audience laughed again.

"And sometimes I'm going to tell you to think big and hit that home run. I call those Reggie Singer Swingers! And my wife says I say things without thinking. She calls those the Reggie Singer Slingers! You know, flinging and slinging stuff and just seeing what sticks to the wall."

Matt laughed and settled back into his seat like a child eating a snack and watching his favorite cartoon.

"Passion is burning desire. Passion drives you to impact the world. Passion is the fuel that burns the midnight oil, pushing you to achieve your goals. Passion has given us the inventions that revolutionized our lives. Anyone can see a problem, but passionate people solve it.

"Passion is the love you bring to your daily work. Your skills might translate into other industries. You could let someone else be the boss and have less stress—"

"No, thank you," Matt whispered to himself.

"But passion will not let another business steal your heart.

"Passion is a competitive advantage. Your unpassionate competitors? Their tasks are mundane obligations, placing them into chains. When you are passionate, spending time on your business frees you and breaks the chains that have kept you from rising."

Matt thought about Juan Perez's inspirational advice.

Someone clapped and said, "Amen," like they were in church.

Reggie widened his eyes in a comical expression. "We might have to pass an offering plate—"

The crowd roared.

"—to bail out some of your bad business decisions."

"I'll take that money!" someone yelled out from the back.

Reggie waved his hands, signaling the crowd to simmer down.

"Who are several businesspeople you look up to?" Reggie went silent, staring over the crowd like a schoolteacher searching for a cheating student.

Matt thought of Juan again. He also thought of Allan's wisdom in investing money.

"Did you just answer the question?"

A few people answered, "Yes."

"Why do you look up to them? You admire their passion, don't you? It's the love between a person and their business. Is there an enigmatic twinkle in their eyes? Is a spark lit from the enthusiasm in their words as they discuss what they love doing the most? Don't their words make other people around them pay attention and listen?

"You might sit here and think, 'Do I really need passion?' Investors are seeking entrepreneurs with passion. Imagine a man or woman who does not love their work. Will he execute his operations well? Will she inspire her employees with an emotional paycheck? What are the chances they will make it big? Wise financial investors know that if you have passion, then your heart and soul are attached to your work.

"Passion is like nuclear power. Use passion well, and you can light up cities and countries, provide electricity to millions of people, and improve their lives. Misuse passion—" Reggie made a bomb sound and threw his arms over his head like they exploded. "—and even you will be burnt in its blaze."

Reggie's voice rose in fervor like a preacher. "Passion keeps you ahead of the curve. It is the driving force behind being the best and not merely better. It gives you determination to do whatever it takes to get to the top. It sharpens your creativity, so you think out of the box. It drives you to find problems that no one else realized were hampering productivity and efficiency. It compels you to create innovative solutions to problems that others deemed unsolvable."

"Listen to me. Being an entrepreneur differs from being an employee. Employees have their duties determined by others. As an entrepreneur, you will establish your own objectives that are backed by the activities and strategies you develop. How will you put those strategies into action?"

Doubt crept into Matt's mind. Did he know how to establish strategies? Did he know how to start it all?

"Do you fear failing?"

The question unnerved Matt. He had never feared failing. He looked at the people who sat around him. He thought about some of the investors he had seen in the hotel hallways. They were people who had giant online followings and ginormous portfolios. A startup in Grant City, Indiana, felt small and insecure. The feeling of uncertainty was new and unwelcoming.

"Address failure! Address obstacles! No matter how cautious and forward-thinking you are, you will encounter obstacles and difficulties along the route. You can never achieve the success you desire if the little things make you doubt your choice to launch your own business. Keep your thoughts optimistic by shutting down the fear of failure. Concentrate on achieving the goal.

"Are you patient? Sometimes, passion works against patience. There are no shortcuts to growth. You must put in long hours every day and night before your endeavors are rewarded. Few people can maintain this dedicated level of concentration without immediate reward. You may work for years without getting compensated because the revenue your company creates might be allocated to accelerating its expansion.

"Success requires patience. Are you ready to give up your short-term gratification for long-term outcomes?

"Just keep this in mind: if you succeed, your business will pay you more every day than your buddies who are employees earn in their biweekly paychecks.

"Do you hear me? That's at least ten times more!"

Matt moved to the edge of his seat, leaning forward to hear the truth. He imagined making ten times more than Kevin. What if he hit it really big and could buy his old company and fire Kevin? His old coworkers would cheer as they ushered Kevin to the door.

"You can succeed if you are a problem solver. Will customers see your passion when their problems arise? Can you provide solutions that are tailored to their unique concerns?"

Yes! Matt wanted the prize. He wanted the success. He pushed away the fears. If these great investors excelled in large markets, he surely could excel in a medium-sized market.

"Think about what you are embarking on as you contemplate starting a business. Are you prepared to put in years of nonstop work to realize your dreams?"

Yes!

"Do you have that passion?"

Yes!

"Do you have the passion to succeed that can drive you through the challenges you will face?"

Yes!

"When you're knee-deep in the muck of starting a business, will passion push you through?"

Yes!

"When in the moment you want to quit, will your passion drive you? Will you remember the goal and the benefits and realize that it will be worth tackling the difficulties and negotiating the compromises?"

Matt believed! He believed he could rise. He pumped his fist in the air. The audience applauded. A few whistled.

Reggie's arms flailed in the air. "Thank you! Passion is only the start."

"You need Resources. Resources stand for time, money, and people. Who do you need on your team? How much time will you give this business to get off the ground? How much money will you infuse to get it started? How much money do you need to make in the timeframe you set?

"You need Inspiration. You must have a strong company culture. Define values, purpose, and goals. Create a mission statement that will guide decisions and actions. If your employees understand your company's purpose, they will be more motivated to work hard and achieve their goals.

"You need Stems. They will make you productive and effective. Document your processes. Tell employees how to complete a task. Tell them the policies to govern the process. Give them consistency. Systems will reduce costly errors.

"You need Engagement. You need to expand your business and increase sales. Communicate effectively with customers and employees. Convey clear messages. Build strong relationships. Increase loyalty and drive growth!

"You can rise! Have passion! And then get your Resources, Inspiration, Systems, and Engagement sorted out! See you at the book signing and the panel discussion." Reggie left his microphone on the podium, grabbed his shades, held up a peace sign, and walked off the stage.

Suddenly it was over. Matt wasn't even sure of what Reggie said right at the end. His mind had been swept away to a life of success, not working for Kevin, a rejuvenated Grant City, a heritage that honored his mom and dad, and the freedom of being his own boss!

CHAPTER 5

The Book Signing

At Reggie's book signing, Matt wanted a picture. As he waited in line, he watched Reggie interact with people. Reggie wore reading glasses instead of shades, looking up and over them to converse. At the keynote speech, he had the aura of a rock star preacher. Sitting at the table, he seemed more like a wise uncle, maybe even like Allan.

When it was his turn, Matt walked up to Reggie and handed him the book. "I'm ready to RISE. I'm already rising."

Reggie raised his eyebrows. "Where?"

"Grant City, Indiana."

Reggie looked up from signing the book. "That's ambitious. Heard that region was once the steel capital of the Midwest. That place could use a revival."

"I'm going to do it!"

Reggie lowered his head and looked up over his glasses at Matt. "You?"

Matt's heart slumped. Reggie didn't have the same infectious enthusiasm at the table. "You don't think I can do it? Is that a Reggie Singer Stinger?"

"No. Not by yourself. You said, 'I'm going to do it.' Do you have a team? Do you have people who are resources for your company? You don't want to be your own resource. That's ground level."

Matt bit the inside of his cheek.

"Have you read this?" Reggie held up the book.

"Twice. With highlights and notes." Matt motioned to the book. "Not that copy. That copy is a collectible, a souvenir. I was hoping you would write something in it that I can look back on."

Reggie opened the book and thumped the top of the inside cover where Matt had already written "Leadership vs. Dictatorship" in thick capital letters. "What's the story behind this?"

"Kevin."

"Is he a leader who inspired you or a dictator who inspired you?"

"Dictator. Used to work for him. He didn't understand customers. Wasted a lot of my ideas. Never admitted when he was wrong. Yelled a lot. He…" Matt searched for a nicer word than the ones he was thinking, "…accelerated my departure from my former company and into my own company."

"Been there. Are you a visionary?"

"Definitely."

"You have an integrator?"

"I guess it's my sister."

"You guess? Did you bring her, too?"

"No."

Reggie seemed to shake and nod his head at the same time, looking like it made his head spin. "What's your name?"

"Matt."

"I'll write an inspirational message for you." Reggie wrote light and fast, the sound of his pen like someone slashing a sword in the air. He closed the book, handed it to Matt, and extended his hand.

Matt shook it. "Thanks, Reggie!"

"We'll see you soon, won't we?"

"What? Why?" Matt laughed.

"Two years." Reggie didn't smile.

"Seriously?" Matt smirked, hoping to get Reggie to smile.

Reggie nodded.

"Why then?"

"Because that's when it will hit you." Reggie's voice was cold and sober. At that table, Reggie wasn't funny or charismatic. His voice carried the cold frost of hard realities.

Matt's voice felt a little dry. "What will hit me?"

"Next." Reggie waved over the next person in line. "It was nice meeting you, Matt."

Matt walked away, partly confused, replaying the conversation in his mind. He hadn't impressed Reggie. For a moment, he doubted himself. Second time today. This was new territory for Matt.

Matt shook his head clear of the doubt and cracked the book to read Reggie's message. Underneath "Leader or Dictator?" Reggie had written a message in equally large capital letters.

"RESOURCES, MATT! RESOURCES!!!

That's a Reggie Singer Finger pointing you in the right direction.

-Reggie"

CHAPTER 6

The Failure

Matt pulled at his hair with both hands. "I don't understand, Charlotte. Why are you trying to hire people? What does this have to do with you finding deals for us?"

"Listen, Matt!" Charlotte's face tensed, and her jaw pushed forward. "We've been at this for two years—"

"And don't forget you begged—actually Allan begged—for you to be part of this."

Charlotte mock laughed. "That's a selective memory, Matthew! For two years, you haven't given me much to do. I get a paycheck. I'm the one who started wholesaling because the rentals aren't bringing in enough."

"Yes! You started that behind my back, Char!"

"Behind your back! Are. You. Serious." Hands on hips, Charlotte swore at him.

"Whoa! Where is that language coming from?"

"From frustration. From not being included. From having next to nothing to do. So I found something to do, and it's making more money than what we set out to do. And you're accusing me of doing it behind your back!"

Matt fumed. He had no response because she was right. But he didn't want to admit it.

Charlotte poked him in the chest. "I can make a difference. If you won't let me, I'm leaving."

"So you can match curtains and couches in people's houses?"

"No. I'll buy the houses, flip them myself, and beautifully match the curtains and couches for the pics in my listings."

Matt shook his head and then massaged his temples. His voice relaxed. "You find deals for us. You find good deals, Charlotte. You are important." He sighed. "I don't want you to leave. I mean, you create the most attractive and reputable bandit signs in Grant City."

Charlotte slapped her side. "Is that what someone in my position should be doing?"

Matt shrugged.

"Do you even know my position? My title?"

"Yes."

"What is it?"

"Ummmm…it's C-something-O. I forget what we landed on for the middle letter."

"Are you serious?" It wasn't quite a yell, but it was a lot of volume for Charlotte.

"Let's go talk to Allan. Let's see what he says about money."

Matt led the march to Allan's office.

Allan swiveled from his computer and faced them. "Bringing your fight in here?"

"Do you know my title?" Charlotte smacked the desk as she sat down.

"The title we gave you? Or the title that describes what Matt allows you to do?"

"Go easy on me, guys." Matt raised his hands in surrender and didn't sit down.

Allan said, "In title, you're the COO. In practice, Matt doesn't trust you, so he's the COO."

Matt sneered. "Man, you are really confident when Charlotte is in the room. You don't talk like this without her around."

Allan shrugged and turned back to Charlotte. In practice, you are more like a Chief Sales Officer. But with your developing acquisitions skills, you are more like a Chief Product Officer."

"See." Charlotte glared at Matt. "You don't know what I am. You won't let me fulfill my title."

"Allan, we are here because Charlotte wants to hire a salesperson. Can you authorize it for her?"

"Will you let me?"

"Let you what?"

"Authorize it." Allan's hands flailed. "You told me two weeks ago that you have to authorize all the expenditures."

"No. That's your decision to make."

Charlotte snorted.

Allan laughed. "Do you not remember saying that?"

Matt held his hands up in surrender. "Okay. Here's what we'll do because I have to leave and—"

Barb, the secretary, knocked on the metal door frame. "106 North Glendale has a toilet clog."

"Come on, Barb," Matt snarled. "Call the plumber."

Barb popped her bubble gum. "Sheesh. Why didn't I think of that? Or maybe I did, and he said that we're behind on our payments and isn't going to do this one."

Matt held out his hands to Allan. "Why wasn't this paid?"

Allan started to speak, but Barb interjected, "You told me to send you the bill because you wanted to check on the pricing yourself and compare it with some other plumbers before we used them again. Did you do that, Matt?"

"Check the prices?"

"Yes, and give Allan the bill to pay."

Matt groaned. "No. Listen. I'll go unclog the toilet. 802 Glendale, right?"

"106 North Glendale," Barb answered.

"Oh!" The address made Matt pause. "That's Mrs. Burks' house by the movie theater."

"Yes. Your old neighborhood." Barb snapped her gum once more and retreated to her desk.

"So, did we solve what we came in here for?" Matt asked.

"We solved nothing," Charlotte answered.

"Nothing," Allan repeated.

Charlotte said, "Matt, you shouldn't be unclogging toilets."

"It's okay. I can use the change of pace."

Matt hopped in his old Chevy Silverado and pulled the door shut.

Bang! The door hit the frame. Matt remembered the sagging door hinge and mumbled as he opened the door slightly, lifted it by the interior handle, and pulled it shut.

Charlotte walked up to the car, and Matt lowered the window.

"Time for a new truck?"

"Wouldn't be a wise investment of money." Matt fired up the car and revved the engine, hoping Charlotte would get the hint that he didn't want to talk.

"You okay?" She patted his shoulder.

"I just need to unclog the toilet."

"Anything else stopped up? In you?"

Matt pulled his lips tight. "This truck is great. Still holds the tools in the back."

"I see. You don't want to talk. May I just say one thing?"

Matt revved the engine.

"Please."

Matt nodded and let off the gas pedal.

"You shouldn't be the one handling the tools, the plungers. Anyway, I called Plumber Stan. He said he would go do it."

"Plumber Stan has the hots for you."

"Maybe." Charlotte giggled. "Maybe I took advantage of that to get a favor for my brother. Maybe we've gone on a date."

Matt gasped. "With Plumber Stan? What do you see in him?"

"Strong hands." Charlotte bit her lip.

Matt gasped even louder. "How would you know?" He shook his head. "Never mind. Call Plumber Stan and tell him not to go. It's good for me. It clears my head."

"If we were in a situation where you didn't have to unclog toilets, your head would be clear. If we were in a situation where you didn't feel you had to approve expenditures, your head would be clear. How…"

Charlotte's voice trailed off.

"How what?"

"Matt…How did we get here?"

"I want freedom. I want to rehab Grant City, our old neighborhood."

"You can't redeem the past by redeeming old houses."

Matt's eyes shot daggers at her. He revved the engine. The RPMs shot to 6000. "I'll see you in two days when I get back from Miami. When U-Up invests again with us, I'll give you money for a salesperson."

CHAPTER 7

The Tenant

Plumber Stan was already on the job when Matt pulled up to Miss Burks' house at 106 North Glendale. Matt knocked on the front door, and Mrs. Burks answered.

"Well, hello, Matthew!" Though she was slightly hunched over, Miss Burks beamed. Compassion warmed Matt's heart as she bent her head up to look him in the eye. She spoke with a southern drawl, one of the many transplants from Mississippi whose families had come to work in the steel mills.

"Why are you still here, Mrs. Burks? I thought you'd be gone by now."

"You making fun of my age?" She playfully swatted at Matt.

"No. I mean, I know a lot of people who went back to family in Mississippi."

She held up a finger and started into a lecture Matt had heard at least a half dozen times before. "That's where I came from. Grant City is where I am. This is my community. This is my people. My neighbors are my people. My church is my people. You are my people." She grabbed his hands in hers.

"In all seriousness, are you doing okay?"

Miss Burks pulled her hands away from Matt. "Don't come around here trying to tell me I don't have to pay my rent this month. You've tried that before, and I'm not a charity case."

"I don't think you are."

"I told you. I've forgiven Gerald for leaving me. I've forgiven my daughter for what she stole from me. God provides, Matthew."

Matt shook his head. "Do you need anything?"

"You know what I need? I need my prayer answered. The young folks in this neighborhood need a place to play. The Hub Playground has fallen apart. Addicts shoot up in that old theater on Broadway. I know Gloria is there sometimes. I stay here hoping she'll get sober someday." Her words were replaced by tears. "I remember when you lived a few blocks over and were close with James. You two would always play hoops. You pushed each other. He'd say, 'Nana, Matt makes me want to be a better person.'"

"I don't know that I've ever had as good a friend as James."

"This place wasn't like that then. Well, until he was shot. That's when it started."

"I'm trying to help it change back, Miss Burks."

"I know you're trying, Matthew. Everyone who has eyes and ears knows that you are trying to help."

Plumber Stan entered from the basement and held up a corroded pipe.

Matt looked at Stan's hands and scowled.

"You okay, Mr. Wellington?" Stan asked. "This pipe is just one of several changes I'm making. I'll be right back inside, Mrs. Burks. Just going out to my van."

Matt followed Stan to the van. "I was going to do it."

Stan opened the van door and started clawing through a bin of metal parts. "I know, Mr. Wellington."

"Call me Matt."

Stan nodded, and his mop of curly hair fell over his forehead. He took a hat from the rack in his van and put it on. "Yes, sir."

"Thank you, Stan. Do we still owe you for other jobs?"

"Ummm...yes, but it's not 30 days yet. Nothing's late."

"Barb had called me about several other jobs, but I am in the middle of a large job at the high school."

"So why are you able to do this one?"

Stan nervously laughed.

"Charlotte?"

Stan turned red. "Are you—"

Someone pounded on the back of the van. A woman's voice shouted. "Why you here, Matt?"

Matt recognized the voice immediately. It was Gloria, Mrs. Burks' daughter. Her vocal chords had been thrashed by a lifetime of substance abuse and screaming.

Gloria got in Matt's face, wagging her finger. "Why don't you get out of here instead of making it too expensive to live here? We're okay without you around! I don't want you here anymore!"

"Gloria!" Mrs. Burks had appeared on her porch, holding a broom like it was an axe. "Get away from him. Get away from Matthew. He didn't do anything. You know that. He's doing good to everyone here."

"Shut up, Mama! Shut up!" Gloria started towards her mother's porch.

Mrs. Burks raised the broom like she was ready to battle.

Gloria stopped and shooed away her mother. "Forget you. I'll forget you the way you forget me and James."

Gloria stormed away.

Miss Burks' eyes and lips were pulled tight as she watched every step of Gloria stomping to the corner. "I'm sorry you had to see that, Matthew. Keep doing what you do." She retreated into the house.

"I had my pipe wrench ready in case you needed backup!" Stan waited a beat and then laughed.

"Second time today, you would have helped me out."

"Is Mrs. Burks the grandma of Jimmy Burks?" Stan asked.

"Yes."

"Jimmy's mom is mad at you for what happened?"

Matt swallowed. "I went to the movie with him the night he got shot outside the theater. It could have been me. Just stray gunfire from new gangs."

Stan retrieved a pipe piece and closed the van door. "I was still in second grade when that happened. It changed a lot. It changed how a lot of people felt about this city."

"It changed how I felt about the city, too. I wanted out even quicker, but once I got out, I wanted to do something to help. It changes you. Seeing your buddy bleeding out...not knowing what to do...knowing that it could have been you."

"Can I be honest, Mr. Wellington?"

"Yes, but it's Matt."

"I forgot. I know you haven't paid a few bills, and I know I went on a date with your sister, but I mostly came today because I know what you are trying to do in Grant City, and I believe you can do it."

"Umm...wow! Thanks."

"Charlotte thinks the world of you. On our first date, she just talked about you and Allan. Made me a little insecure, to be honest."

"How many dates have you been on?"

"I stopped counting after five."

"Wait! What?"

Stan sheepishly grinned.

Matt turned to his car. "Thanks, Stan! I'm flying out to Miami. Hopefully, I'll get some more investor money tomorrow. Then we can pay you."

CHAPTER 8

The Investor

Matt knew he was fortunate to get a last-minute meeting with Urban Upscale Properties. Lesser known as UUP, they were more known as "U-Up," and their marketing slogan was "You Up for the Fix Up?" U-Up invested in rehabbing properties and extending charity to the communities. They started in Miami, hit it big in New Orleans after Hurricane Katrina, and spread to Atlanta, Charlotte, and Nashville.

U-Up had invested in twenty of NGC's properties. Ten fix-and-flips and ten rentals. When Matt started his business, U-Up was expanding into other states. Matt's initial networking with them was through Juan Perez in Chicago, but now he had to keep the relationship alive.

Matt felt refreshed as he drove his rental car towards the Atlantic Ocean. It was one thing to have offices in Miami, it was another to cross the causeway over the Biscayne Bay and head towards South Beach. The U-Up offices were on the seventh floor of an office building that looked west towards downtown Miami.

A secretary ushered Matt into a meeting promptly at 8:00 p.m.

"Thank you for fitting me in at this time of night," Matt bowed to a woman whose deep tan and short bleach-blond hair hid her age.

She wore a white suit with a black t-shirt beneath. "I'm Valentina. But call me Val. It was fate that you called. We had been wanting to talk to you."

Matt stopped in his tracks. "About what?"

"Let's hear what you want first?" Val motioned to a white leather couch that faced floor-to-ceiling windows. She lowered the lights in the office. The sun had started its descent in the west, turning the skyline into a silhouette of tall buildings against a swirl of pastels in the sky. "Would you like a drink?

"No. But thank you." Matt sat on the opposite end of the U-shaped couch and leaned forward. "I'm looking for more capital and am asking you to invest."

"No!"

Her quick answer shocked Matt. "Okay. That's it? I traveled here just for this. You won't hear my pitch?"

"No." She smiled. "I have something else to talk about. U-Up really likes you, Matt. I personally like what I've heard about you. The partners like what they've seen of 'Mr. Wellington,' from the brief interactions and your social media platform."

"Then why not invest?"

"We don't love your business model. To us, you're the right guy in the wrong seat."

"I don't understand."

"You have every intangible to succeed. You aren't exactly succeeding in your current situation, are you?"

"Yes, I am."

"Then why are you here asking us for money?"

"Expansion."

Val playfully rolled her eyes as she laughed. "Matthew...may I call you Matthew? Matthew Wellington is a name that shines with success."

"What's your middle name?"

"Harris."

"Wow! Matthew Harris Wellington. Now that is regal."

"Thank you."

"Matthew, your business model is that you are taking houses in your hometown and converting them into something affordable for the people who already live there."

"No."

"Isn't that what you are doing? Be honest."

"I'm creating revenue and reviving the area."

"U-Up raises entire neighborhoods to upscale neighborhoods. The second U in our name *is* for upscale. You haven't done this. You've raised prices a little bit, but you haven't moved the needle on the neighborhoods as we would like to see in our business model."

"Is the point to drive out who lives there?"

Val leaned forward. "No. We try to buy many houses in concentrated areas and raise the entire area. We don't drive people out. We buy empty properties and bring new people in. We make the area and the houses better, and more money comes into the neighborhood. It raises everyone in the community."

"I don't have the capital to buy larger blocks of homes."

"Exactly! You're in the wrong seat. Your strategy is different from our strategy. Two years ago, when we invested, we were investigating different strategies. We've learned that our focused strategy is king. Our investment in you is not worth repeating."

"You invested three million dollars. You make it sound like it's nothing."

Val walked to the window and pointed towards downtown Miami. "There are neighborhoods west beyond those buildings and north of those whose property values have escalated by hundreds of thousands of dollars because of U-Up. We can make three million dollars on one or two smart deals here in South Beach. I'm not trying to be harsh or condescending, but Grant City is the minor leagues compared to what we do. Our investment was negligible, an experiment that we don't want to repeat."

"So what do you want me to do?"

"We want to expand our model. West to Dallas. North along I-95. Also, into the Midwest. We want you to head up our efforts in Chicago."

"Bad memories."

"Of Chicago?"

"Yes. Bad bosses. Low ceilings."

"We'll be great bosses. We have a model you follow. As long as you follow it, you won't even realize that you have a boss."

"I'm happy where I am."

"I don't believe you, Matt."

"There's something I want more than a lot of properties. What do you personally want, Val?"

"We want to afford a building that looks east over the Atlantic Ocean."

"You're doing all of this for an office on the opposite side of the building?"

"No. We're doing it for our own building closer to the ocean. A few blocks that way." Val pointed east. "We all have different goals, Matt. Those are our business goals. We value excellence. What do you value?"

Matt started and stopped a few times. He drew his face tight as he thought. "I value...." His voice trailed off. "Redeeming Grant City?"

Val sat down next to him and patted his knee. "That's a goal, not a value. May I step out of the 'trendy-high-level-executive-in-a-beautiful-office' role for a moment?"

"Of course."

"Matt, I'm old enough to be your mother. I've been in REI for a long time. When I started, mortgage rates were double digits. At U-Up, everyone on the executive board has a charity that our company essentially funds. Mine is a woman's shelter a few miles from here. U-Up pays for the entire operation. Those ladies need help. I want them to be redeemed."

"Then you understand me."

"Yes. But you don't understand the business. We can make compassionate and redemptive impacts because neither of those is part of our business model. We improve the world. We improve people's lives by creating upscale urban properties. We are well paid, and we are very generous in areas we each are passionate about."

"I don't know if I agree about that not being part of my business model."

"That's fine. But when you leave here, compare the dozens of people you are helping with the tens of thousands we are helping in our charities across America. You will be empowered to help so many more people with a tougher business model."

"So, are we done?"

"May I have one more minute? After all, you came here just for this meeting."

"Of course."

"You will easily make seven figures your first year. In a few years, as you build bigger, you can start a charity in Grant City. No one would be opposed to that."

"I don't want to go back to Chicago."

"One more offer, then. Indianapolis. We want to go there, too. You wouldn't have to move states. It's not seven figures to start, but you can work up to it. Think about it."

"So, it's a hard no to investing in my current model?"

"Correct. We like you. However, we have no desire to fund you treading water when you could be driving a yacht." Val smiled. "If we had this meeting in a few years when we have a building that faces the ocean, I would have pointed to one on the Atlantic."

CHAPTER 9

The Meltdown

The early morning flight landed in Indianapolis. Anyone looking at Matt's red eyes at 6:30 in the morning after a two-hour flight would have assumed he was tired.

But he had been crying.

Something broke on that plane ride home. For two years, he had built New Grant City Properties. He never took "no" for an answer. Not from an investor. Not from a seller. Not from a contractor.

But Urban Upscale Investors said "no."

As he drove away from the airport towards the city, Matt considered the modest Indianapolis skyline. U-Up's job offer wasn't that far from Grant City.

Matt shut down the thoughts of anything other than New Grant City. His heart was invested. His money was invested.

After two years of NGC, could the thought of not having to be *the* boss appeal to him? He wouldn't find funding. He'd find deals and contractors and never have issues paying them. He wouldn't have family ties to consider in his business decisions. He could be a cold, hard businessman and drive his way to success and prosperity. Maybe do it for ten years, build a financial portfolio and a reputation, and then restart NGC in his early-to-mid forties.

When he finally reached the border of Grant City, Matt wasn't sure where to drive. He didn't want to stop at home and have Jean ask him how the trip went. He didn't really want to have Charlotte and Allan see him crestfallen.

A text chimed through his Bluetooth. A text came onto his car display.

"When you coming in? Emergency! - Allan"

Matt drove down Broadway and looked at the dilapidated storefronts he wanted to renovate. He thought of the *Cars* movie that his toddler son loved watching over and over. An old town brought back to life. The stout brick buildings on Broadway once housed five-and-dimes and diners, record stores, and barbershops. Their storefront windows had been filled with flyers for community events. Now, the windows were covered in broken boards.

The next text arrived.

"Contractor on phone. Won't work if we don't pay him today for the last four jobs. -A"

Matt stopped at a traffic light. A woman talking to herself and gesturing to the air crossed in front of him. As his eyes followed her, they latched onto a homeless man pushing himself out of a hole in the boarded-up doors of an abandoned grocery store. An emaciated man pushed a shopping cart filled with empty bottles.

We don't have the money to make this better.

When the light turned green, Matt screeched down the road, fleeing the neighborhoods he wanted to transform. He didn't want to be seen. He had failed them. He was going to renovate this town.

Was. He questioned if it would ever happen.

Maybe U-Up was the next step. It was better than risking going back to a situation where he would work for another Kevin.

Matt made a left onto South Maple Street. Four blocks later, he pulled up in front of three houses NGC was renovating. Each had a dumpster in the driveway, the clock ticking on the garbage company picking up an empty dumpster. None of the houses had anyone working on them. The contractor would have started work by now.

Matt replied to Allan's texts.

"Be there in 10."

When Matt made it to NGC, he sat in the idling car. He wanted to rehearse what he would say, but he couldn't put consecutive thoughts together. He drove back to the alley, parked, and entered the back door.

"Matt!" Allan darted out of his office. "We don't have the money to pay the...."

"The contractors? I know! I know! You just texted that to me."

"No. No." Allan's face soured. "This is for property taxes on one of our buildings. Did you...get the money from U-Up?"

That question lit Matt's fuse. "No! No! They didn't like our business model."

"I'm sorry, Matt." Allan reached to put his hand on Matt's shoulder, but Matt shrugged it away.

Charlotte appeared from her office. She lowered her head. "Matt, if you need cash flow, Plumber Stan told me that his parents are always looking for investments."

"No!"

"I could talk to Lisa about if we can invest more," Allan offered.

"No! Definitely not. You've done plenty, Allan."

"So what should I do, Matt?" Allan asked.

"I'm going to grab my tools and go work on the houses myself. So we can get tenants and pay off the contractors for the other work."

"Have you ever put mud on drywall?" Charlotte stepped in front of her brother. "Your time is more valuable than that."

Matt grunted and stomped into his office. He lifted his computer bag above his head and slammed it down on his desk. He groaned and shoved books off his shelves. He grabbed several books and flung them across the room.

Allan watched in horrified silence.

Charlotte stepped into Matt's office. "Please stop! Please!"

Matt seethed. He picked up a book and slammed it on the desk, breaking the front binding. The cover laid open at an awkward angle like a badly broken bone.

Matt took several deep breaths. "I just—" Matt's thoughts were completely shut down by the inside cover of the book. He caught a glimpse of three words.

Leader

Dictator

Resources

"What's wrong, Matt?" Charlotte's tone was soft. She stepped towards him.

Matt felt like a dictator. He imagined how his old boss, Kevin, would have laughed at his outburst. *Failure* echoed through his mind.

He thought back to Reggie signing the RISE book that now lay broken on the desk.

Resources.

Matt was ready to go drywall his properties when he should be running the company.

"Two years," Matt muttered under his breath. "He said we would need RISE in two years."

"What are you talking about?" Charlotte asked.

Matt looked at his sister with sober eyes. "Do we have any closings in the pipeline?"

"Three."

"How soon will we have any cash?"

"Over ninety-thousand next week."

"I want to bring in a business coach," Matt said.

"Listen," Allan said. "I think that's a great idea. But let me lend us the money. You can pay Lisa and me back next week. I think the coach will be a great reset, but let's not ignore our bills to hire a coach. There are people who need us to pay them. They need to pay their own bills and care for their families."

Charlotte nodded. "I think that's a plan. It beats beating up your office."

CHAPTER 10

The Coach

When Reggie Singer got out of his rental car, he looked a little smaller and thinner than Matt remembered. His movements weren't rushed or hurried with the energy he had two years ago during the Orlando talk. He looked more like the sage who had signed books. He gently closed the driver's door, opened the backseat door, and pulled out a satchel.

The sharp winter sun blinded Matt as he stepped out into the early Grant City morning. "Good morning, Reggie! Thank you for coming. Especially on short notice. I can't believe that it worked out."

"My pleasure." He looked Matt soberly in the eye. "Let's make it a great day for NGC!"

"You love what you do, don't you?"

Reggie thought and nodded. "I love helping people. I'm truly blessed to find an opportunity."

"This way to the conference room." Matt pointed to the back corner of the offices.

Charlotte and Allan were already in the conference room on the right side of the table. After the introductions and offering the head of the table to Reggie, Matt sat on the left. Reggie put his satchel down on the left and plugged in his computer.

"We have all the data you requested." Matt pointed to Charlotte. "Charlotte will cast it onto the TV. What do you want to do first? Payroll? Monthly numbers?"

"Show gratitude." Reggie looked at Charlotte and pursed his lips. He sized up Allan through his thick glasses and then turned his gaze to Matt. "What is something personally that you are grateful for right now?"

Matt reared his head back. "I was hoping to get right down to business. That's not what I thought—"

"Are you going to say it's not what you paid for?"

Matt said nothing.

"I don't care if I get paid. I told you the price. If you don't think my being here for Resource Day is worth it, then you don't have to pay me anything. If you think it was worth half of my asking price, then pay me half. If you think it's worth ten times my asking price, no need to pay more than the asking price."

"I'm sorry. I didn't mean to insult you." Matt lowered his head.

"Good news keeps us balanced and centered. There is more at work here than profits and losses and payroll and acquisitions. There's friction. I felt its heat the moment I walked in. You are sitting four feet from your siblings, but it feels like it could be four miles. Businesses stop being grateful. Relationships stop being grateful."

"I'm thankful you're here." Allan smiled sheepishly. "We need help."

"That's a start, Allan. What else are you thankful for?" Reggie asked.

"Well...." Allan looked to Charlotte and then Allan. "I haven't told you guys yet. I thought we were done, but Lisa is pregnant."

Charlotte hugged him. Matt sat back in his chair and cheered. "That is good news," he said. "I'm really happy for you, Allan."

"Congratulations! Charlotte, how about you?" Reggie asked.

Charlotte blushed. "Agreed to four wholesale acquisitions this week that should translate to cash in a few weeks!" She burst into a smile and pumped her fists into the air.

"Awesome. Awesome. It's a good feeling to have a little cash to operate with." Reggie applauded. "Matt?"

Matt puffed his cheeks and looked to the ceiling. "I'm stealing Allan's first answer. It's good that I called you because nothing has been good lately. Not here. Not at home. We need to change."

"Thank you for saying that. If you don't come to the end of yourself, things won't get better." Reggie scribbled a note. "Second question. What role do you play in the business, and what are you great at?"

"I'm the CEO," Matt straightened up in his chair. "I'm great at setting the agenda and seeing where we need to go?"

"So you're the visionary?"

"Yes."

"How about you, Charlotte?"

"I'm still not sure."

"Come on, Char! You're the COO!" Matt tapped his palm on the conference table, allowing his dissatisfaction to slowly dissipate.

"So, you got the middle letter right this time?" Char looked to Reggie. "Technically, I'm the COO. But Matt takes too much on him and makes COO decisions. I'm starting to think I'm great at finding deals for wholesaling—though that isn't really our goal."

"I'm glad you're getting great at it, Char, or we could never do the rentals." Allan scribbled in the air. "Money is all over the place."

Reggie whistled. "Can't wait to see your P&Ls. So you're saying that acquisitions is making money and rentals and flips isn't?" He looked at Charlotte and Allan. They both looked at Matt. "Is that true, Matt?"

Matt never looked down. He looked Reggie right in the eye. "It's kinda true. It's not making the money we thought it would. Char's wholesale deals have kept us afloat."

"We'll straighten this out. What about you, Allan? What's your job?"

"I'm the CFO. I keep the books."

"And what are you great at, Allan?"

Charlotte jumped in before Allan could answer. "Making babies."

Allan blushed as he chuckled. "It's true. But I think I'm great with numbers. I love numbers."

"Well then! Let's move to question 3 before Charlotte embarrasses you any further. What are the challenges today at NGC that are limiting effectiveness? Let's clear the air a little bit. What do we need to fix? We tend to create silos and kill communication. Let's come out of our corners and talk."

Matt immediately piped up. "I've lost investors. I'm behind on paying contractors. I can't get people in the rentals because the work is unfinished. That about sums it all up." Matt looked at Charlotte and Allan.

"Okay. But I'm going to let them answer for themselves. Allan, what's not working?"

Allan swallowed. "I'm unhappy here."

"What?" Matt shot up from his office chair. "That's not the type of challenge Reggie is talking about!"

Charlotte rose, too. "You haven't noticed he's unhappy?

"Allan, how could you not be happy?"

"I'm stressed. I never have tasks that I complete. I leave work every day with three dozen things hanging over my head, and I know that the next day I'll only get half of those done. The list will keep getting bigger. And some just go away because we ignore them, and I'm wondering why they were on my list to begin with."

Reggie rubbed his hands together. "Wooo! This is getting real. Allan, thank you so much for speaking that and feeling free to speak that. Matt, some of the business problems you talked about...the root causes aren't just business and numbers. Charlotte, what's a challenge?"

She bit her cheek and looked back and forth between her brothers. "Us."

Matt dropped his pen on the table.

"We're not working," she continued. "Allan and I work fine. Matt is working hard, but the sum of it is working. I think there's a lot of pressure here on top of the financials. I sometimes think that Matt is trying to salvage a past in Grant City that has left the building and is gone. The focus waivers. There are days he rallies us around doing our part to improve the city, and then later that day, he's angry over money and gives off a vibe that we're not doing enough as a company."

Matt started to speak but just sighed.

"Okay. Last question," Reggie said. "What do you want to accomplish by the end of today?"

"A path forward," Matt said.

"I agree," Allan said.

"How about you, Charlotte?"

"Two things. I want my brother to respect me."

"Come on, Char," Matt clenched his hands together.

"Let her finish." Reggie motioned for Matt to simmer down. "What's the second one?"

"I want Matt to find peace and joy."

Matt glared at her and then smirked.

"Hot start! And I sense we're barely scratching the surface." Reggie clapped his hands together. "You need to complete the Rise Business Assessment on page 4 of the workbook. Rate NGC on a scale of one to three for each of the four statements from the four quadrants and add them up. Then we will start on Resources."

CHAPTER 11

The Assessment

Reggie approached the whiteboard, looked over the color choices, and picked up a green marker. He drew a diamond with an X through it, dividing the diamond into four quadrants. He then wrote "Resources" in the first quadrant.

"Every business needs to RISE. You have to be mature in all of these phases to RISE." Reggie emphasized "RISE" as he filled in the other four quadrants on his diamond.

"You need Resources. You need Inspiration. You need Systems. You need Engagement. You don't have to get one done before the other. But you will not be 100% mature until you fulfill each quadrant."

Reggie opened his RISE manual. "From the business assessment, tell me your total for each quadrant. It should be somewhere between four and twelve."

"Allan. Give me your four totals."

Allan cleared his throat and looked out of the side of his eyes at Matt. "Resources 6. Inspiration 8. Systems 4. Engagement 4."

"Char?" Reggie motioned to her.

"Resources 5. Inspiration 4. Systems 5. Engagement 8.

Reggie sat back. "Whoo! Some big differences there. Matt, you go ahead."

"Resources 8. Inspiration 7. Systems 4. Engagement 7."

Reggie tallied the numbers. "So, your total numbers are Resources 19, Inspiration 19, Systems 13, and Engagement 19. That averages six-six-four-six."

"Can I debate the numbers?" Matt asked.

"No," Reggie answered tersely as he flipped the page in the manual. "It's a metric for now. Look at page 5. It's about plateaus. Matt, has NGC plateaued?"

"Absolutely. We don't know what to do next. I hate saying it, but I don't know what to do next."

"That sounds like a plateau, doesn't it, Allan?"

"Yes, sir."

"And as the CFO, you are sitting around day to day, hour by hour, waiting for Matt to tell you what to do next, right? You're waiting for the next change that visionary Matt is going to make so he can conquer that plateau."

"Basically. You just summed up my job. Matt has given me a title, but not accountability."

Reggie smiled at Allan. "Thank you for your honesty. You will plateau. There are adjustments you make to grow. The adjustments have to be in rhythm with each other. How have your adjustments been going, Matt?"

"Well, since we're being super transparent and vulnerable today—"

"That's your favorite!" Charlotte interjected.

Matt laughed. "Right, Char. Well, Reggie, I feel like a failure. I'm stuck."

"Listen to me, Matt. I've helped hundreds of businesses. It's not a question of 'Will you get stuck?' You will get stuck. When we get stuck, we leave our system of what works. We wander through a room, looking for a light switch. Our new system can become so complex that it doesn't work anymore. We must reduce complexity."

Allan cleared his throat. "This resonates with me. We've overcomplicated everything. Everything is undefined. Those employees sitting in the cubicles are confused. I think our investors are confused. I invested in this company at the start, yet I'm not sure what exactly we are doing. I thought we were improving houses and neighborhoods through renovations and rentals. Now we're wholesaling. Char's good at it. It's given several employees something to do. Or else they would do nothing."

"But we are going to figure this out, guys." Matt stood and paced. "We're going to simplify. We're going to focus on one area if that's what it takes."

"Matt, it encourages me to hear you say that." Reggie started writing on the board again. "Some people are married to their expectations when they need to move on from them. Let me show you a different acronym for RISE. This is what you need to do to simplify and then grow."

"First, there's Research. Research how your time, money, and man hours are consumed. For instance, how much time do you need for this product or business to be self-sustaining? How much money do you have to invest? Where are you spending your money?"

"I is for Implementation. You implement profit, structure, and purpose.

"S is for Streamline. You streamline processes, procedures, and policies.

"Lastly, E is for Expansion. You expand through branding, succession, and automation. When you leave expansion, you are in a healthy business. Today, we need to work on your time, money, and people resources."

Matt reached for a water bottle. "This repeats a little of what Charlotte said. I was convicted very early in this process. We've been powered by dreams and can-do and chutzpah."

"It's my turn to be honest." Allan's face fell. "I'm afraid. I'm afraid of all of this. That we can't do it. I've got another baby coming. It hurts to think that twenty-seven months ago, we were sitting in the diner finalizing this, but we've invested so much energy…and to hear you admit we haven't been efficient…that's really hard, Matt. I only have so much to give."

"Allan, I am truly sorry. I sold you on me, but I haven't been knowledgeable enough."

Reggie chimed in. "Matt, I appreciate your honesty. Allan, I appreciate your honesty. Charlotte, I appreciate that you are faithful to your brothers. Can I tell you the four things that keep people from running a healthy business? The first is fear.

Exactly. Fear kills passion. Fear is from a lack of knowledge. Do you know why Matt didn't have fear?"

"Because I didn't even realize what I didn't know." Matt smacked his head.

"That's right. Knowledge has to replace fear. But that doesn't happen right away. You sustain it with faith. Matt has a lot of faith. When he lost faith, that's when you started worrying, Allan. Charlotte, you have great faith in your brothers. We need to find you a spot where your faith is more at the forefront of this business, and everyone out in those cubicles sees it."

Charlotte perked up. "I'd like that."

"It's a little traumatic to talk about why, but I'm afraid of flying," Reggie admitted. "This job requires me to get on a plane several times a week. I learned about how planes work. I researched plane accident stats. Statistically, they are very safe. I'm still afraid, but that knowledge got me back on the plane. I have faith we won't crash.

"The second is mindset. We adjust our mindset so that we believe. Don't keep saying, 'We can't do that.' Say, 'How can we do that?' Ask more questions. Make fewer statements."

"I think he's talking to you." Charlotte elbowed Allan.

"The third component is making the right connections, the ones we need to succeed. It's the hands we shake in life. Your failures have caused us to meet. That's not bad. We're figuratively shaking hands. Honestly, Matt, when you called, I already wanted to meet you."

Matt scrunched his face. "I met you two years ago at a book signing. I doubt you remember it."

"I don't. But do you know why I was so intrigued to come? Last week on Tuesday, Val from U-Up texted me to see what I knew about Matthew Wellington in Grant City, Indiana. I said that I didn't know him and wished I could help her. She said you were having a meeting with her the next night. She was offering you a job."

"She offered you a job, Matt?" Allan asked. "And you didn't tell us? Are you taking it?"

"Whoops!" Reggie playfully covered his mouth. "You didn't tell them?"

"Because I'm not taking the job. There's already instability here. I'm not going to leave NGC and abandon Allan, who has invested a lot and sacrificed a lot of stability."

"Wow. A job with U-Up. Thank you, Matt. That means a lot." Allan fought back tears. "That really does."

Matt glared at his sister. "Go ahead, Char. You haven't commented yet."

"I don't need to say anything. You turning it down says a lot."

A silence of unity settled on the room.

Reggie finally broke the silence. "May I finish this thought about the components? Two days after Val called me about Matthew Wellington, I got a cancellation for today. Fifteen minutes after that cancellation, I received an email with a business inquiry from the same Matthew Wellington."

Allan gasped. "That's crazy."

Reggie grinned. "It's crazy. It's fate. Some might say it's a God thing or karma or the universe. But I knew I had to come. And I came because a lot of handshaking has been going on. I knew Val and U-Up. Matt knew U-Up. Matt had met me. I wrote a book. Matt somehow heard of it. All of them are connections."

"That's amazing," Charlotte said. "I might be a little jealous that I'm not in this part of the story."

"Well, Charlotte, you're new at this and just starting to shake hands. Keep making connections. Ask questions. Ask me. Ask the right people. Utilize those connections. But then you need the right mindset."

Matt raised his hand. "Reggie, can we take a break soon? The last couple of minutes are kind of emotional. It has worn me out."

"Yes. Just let me say the fourth component. It's having the right systems and processes. But if you don't have the first three, the fourth one is irrelevant. It's a great time to break."

CHAPTER 12

The Accountability

"Turn to page 8. Let's jump into resources," Reggie announced.

Matt flipped to page eight. "Talent accountability!"

"I don't even know what this means!" Allan laughed.

Reggie shook his head. There are four elements of talent accountability. We need an organizational chart. We will build one on my Mac." The organizational chart software appeared on the screen.

"Looks like graph paper! I'm suddenly interested," Allan said.

Reggie clicked a few shapes, and a hierarchy began to take shape. "I'll assume Matt is on the top line as the CEO." Reggie drew two boxes below Matt's box and connected them to Matt's box with a line. Reggie typed in the box to the left. "Charlotte, you are here as the COO. And Allan, you are here on the right as the CFO. Now, who comes under here."

"I have an assistant finance secretary," Allan said.

"I have a salesperson, an administrative assistant, and three VAs," Charlotte said.

"So you are over sales and operations?" Reggie asked. "Does anyone else do sales?"

"Matt does," Allan says.

Matt nodded. "I do some deals. And sometimes I oversee sales."

"Because you don't trust her?" Allan asked.

"Sometimes Charlotte needs help," Matt said.

Charlotte snorted. "You don't trust me."

Matt countered, "No! It's not that I just don't trust you—"

"Let's just hold on a minute." Reggie held up his hands. "Look at the organizational chart. I'm not judging your titles. I'm just drawing an accurate chart. Everyone should be on here just once. Matt is the CEO. Charlotte is the COO. Allan is the CFO. Under Allan is an assistant financial secretary. Under Charlotte are the sales rep and three VAs. What do they do?"

"Marketing," Charlotte answered. "Lead generation. Website. Social Media. Things like that."

Reggie added the three positions to the organizational chart. "That's cut and dry. Eight people."

"We left off Barb," Allan added.

"What's her title?" Reggie asked. "Who is she under?"

Allan and Charlotte looked to Matt for the answer. Charlotte held her lips tight like she didn't want to laugh.

Matt felt weighed down by Reggie's firm stare. "Barb answers calls sometimes and emails. She records some things with the county. She goes and meets the inspector sometimes. Sometimes I do. Or Char—"

"Because you tell me last minute," she said. "Tell him that you do it last minute."

Matt shrugged. "Okay. Umm…Barb also takes care of snacks for the break area."

"You forgot to tell Reggie that you had Barb pick up your son from Pre-K last week." Allan grinned at Charlotte.

"Yes. And you forgot to tell Reggie that you put her in a negotiation for a property we ended up losing," Char added.

"Do you need to know more?" Matt asked Reggie.

Reggie huffed. "You didn't answer my question."

"Sure, I did."

"I asked for her title. You told me what she does. The next step is going to be a doozy. What is her title?"

"Oh! I get it. She's the...administrative assistant."

"Who does she report to?"

Matt pointed at Charlotte.

Charlotte pointed at Matt with one hand and Allan with the other. "If I had a third arm, I'd point at myself, too."

"Matt, who should she be reporting to?" Reggie asked.

"Charlotte."

Reggie added Barb to the chart. "Okay. Now, we move on to a process ownership chart. This lists out who is accountable for each process. Would you look at page 10?"

Matt studied the new graphic on the page. It had diamonds in a hierarchy similar to the organizational chart.

"Look at the top left. Who is the innovator? Who casts the visions and grows the business?"

"Definitely, Matt," Allan answered.

"Do you agree, Matt?"

Matt straightened up in his chair. "Yes, Reggie."

"Are you committed to this seat for the next 6-12 months?"

"Yes."

"Do you have a clear understanding of expectations for the role?"

"Yes! I created the role."

"Do you have a clear understanding of the process, procedures, and policies for my role?"

Matt hemmed and hawed. "Well...I understand the process. I often make procedures on the fly. The policy is 'just get it done.'"

"That doesn't sound very clear," Charlotte said.

"He wasn't asking you," Matt snapped.

Charlotte didn't back down. "The question said 'clear understanding.'"

"Last question for Matt," Reggie said. "Are you engaged in the work you are asked to do?"

"Absolutely!"

"Okay, next question for everyone. Who is the Lead? Who leads the process and holds it accountable?"

"Charlotte," Matt answered.

"No way!" Charlotte said.

"Then what do you think you do?" Matt squinted at his sister.

"What do *you think* I do? Matt, you take control of everything. You lead the processes." She sat back in her chair. "This is frustrating."

"You're the COO. Leading the processes and holding it accountable is definitely a COO function!"

"Simmer down, Matt," Allan said. "You swoop in every day and take charge of something else. And from day to day, we don't know if you're still in charge of what you were in charge of yesterday. Don't get mad at Charlotte."

Matt slowly exhaled to relieve the heaviness of his anger.

"Do you need a break?" Reggie asked.

"No," Matt answered.

Reggie typed. "Is it fair to say that you are in this seat sometimes, Matt?"

Matt sighed. "Yes. I'm doing what it takes to keep us afloat."

"Of course you are." Reggie's tone was warm. "But it's got you frustrated. We are aiming for a far better state than being kept afloat. We're aiming to RISE. And we're going to get there with honesty and transparency. That said, Matt, let me ask you the questions."

Matt looked at Reggie and nodded. "Go ahead."

"Are you committed to this seat for the next 6-12 months?"

"Yes and no."

"Explain."

"I'm committed to doing it if necessary to keep us afloat. But if we can implement a good structure, then, no, I don't want to be in that seat."

"Do you have a clear understanding of expectations for the role?"

"Yes. I think I do."

"Do you have a clear understanding of the process, procedures, and policies for your role?"

"No. Those things I do by the seat of my pants."

"Are you engaged in the work you are asked to do?"

"Not at all. It's not what I want to do. I feel I have to do it."

Reggie smiled. "Thank you for being honest and transparent. Your turn, Charlotte."

"Are you committed to this seat for the next 6-12 months?"

"Yes."

"Do you have a clear understanding of expectations for the role?"

"Sort of. I understand what is expected for the role, but not necessarily what is expected of me."

"That's fair," Matt said.

Reggie asked, "Do you have a clear understanding of the process, procedures, and policies for your role?"

"Not at all. We don't have any," Charlotte answered.

"That's fair, too," Allan said.

"It is," Matt said.

"Are you engaged in the work you are asked to do?" Reggie asked.

"Yes."

"Thank you," Reggie smiled. "Allan, it's your turn."

"Are you committed to this seat for the next 6-12 months?"

Allan hesitated. Matt's chest felt tight. He rolled his chair away from the table as though he needed space to breathe. He leaned forward, bewildered that his brother had hesitated.

Allan locked eyes with Matt. "Yes."

"Committed?" Reggie verified.

"Yes. You said six months."

"Reggie said six to twelve," Matt said.

"You never know where life will take you with a new baby," Allan said.

Matt sat back in his seat. That was just Allan being Allan, answering out of fear.

"Do you have a clear understanding of expectations for the role?"

"Definitely. I handle the money."

Reggie asked, "Do you have a clear understanding of the process, procedures, and policies for your role?"

"Pretty much."

"Why 'pretty much' and not 'yes?'" Reggie asked.

Allan looked to the ceiling for the answer. "I have a title, but not accountability."

Matt started to speak but held his tongue.

"Let's move on," Reggie said.

"Are you engaged in the work you are asked to do?" Reggie asked.

"No. My work here has lots of drama and dynamics that I don't care for."

Matt rolled his eyes and then dropped his head in his hands.

"Do you have an objection, Matt?" Reggie asked.

"He's just demonstrating the drama that Allan doesn't care for," Charlotte said.

Matt raised his head and shot daggers at her. "No objections, your honor."

"Let's go to the third line: management. Who manages the team and holds them to process? What process should we start with?"

"Property management." Allan rubbed his hands together. His giddy laugh drew Matt's stare.

"What's so funny," Reggie asked.

"It best makes the point," Allan answered.

"Hmmm. That's passive-aggressive, Allan. I see where you are going," Reggie smiled at Allan with admiration. "Who oversees the process of property management?"

"I do." Charlotte raised her hand.

"Who sits in the seat of collections underneath you, Charlotte?"

"Sometimes Barb. Sometimes Matt."

Reggie typed on his computer and filled names into the diamonds. "So…I see Matt, the CEO is over you as the COO, and you are over him as he collects money?"

Charlotte laughed, "Yes. According to this, when Matt is a resource in collections, I am his boss. I like this!"

"So last week," Allan perked up, "Matt went to fix a toilet. So CEO Matt is over COO Charlotte who is over Plumber Matt?"

"Exactly!" Reggie laughed. "Matt is sitting in a lot of seats."

"In this case, it's a toilet seat," Charlotte said, and everyone except Matt laughed. "Come on, Matt, you want to laugh."

"You're clever, Char, but I'm not laughing," Matt tightened his lips.

When Charlotte laughed again, Matt tried to hold in his laugh, but he ended up spraying the table with saliva.

"That's gross," Charlotte chuckled.

"Hey, COO Charlotte," Allan said, "order Janitor Matt to come wipe down the table."

"Okay. Okay. I get it. I'm sitting in too many seats." Matt turned to Reggie. "Can you save me?"

"I'll try, but I need to ask you the questions. Are you committed to the maintenance seat for the next six to twelve months?"

Matt chuckled. "Absolutely not."

"Do you have a clear understanding of expectations for the role?"

"It's that you want the toilet to be able to flush," Allan joked.

Matt sneered at his brother. "I do."

Reggie asked, "Do you have a clear understanding of the process, procedures, and policies for your role?"

"Yes."

"Are you engaged in the work you are asked to do?" Reggie asked.

"Not at all," Matt said. "Okay. I get the point. I shouldn't be sitting in this seat."

"Correct! It's going to take some thinking through, but we're going to define the core processes of NGC. This includes everyone's roles and responsibilities. Once we have that settled, we can ask the four questions of process commitment and consider if we have the right people in the right seat."

"So we are clarifying which seats we need?" Matt asked.

"Exactly. For instance, I think you need a person who does boots-on-the-ground acquisitions. It's someone who reports to Charlotte and is getting sales. She has someone reporting to her who does dispositions. You need a Project Manager who will oversee the collections, turns, leasing, evictions, and maintenance. Right now, it sounds like Matt is the project manager."

"But how do we pay for that?" Allan asked.

"We'll talk about that in a little bit," Reggie said. "We have a few things to work out before we get to the budget. Let's break for lunch."

CHAPTER 13

The Resource Plan

"That was a delicious lunch." Reggie moved to the front of the conference room and stood in front of the TV. "Here's how we're going to spend the second half of the day. We're going to make this chart and create actionable steps to address the weaknesses I hear you revealing. So here are two questions. One: what's the question that hangs over you in this business? Two: What do you need?"

"I'll go first," Matt said. "The question that hangs over me is 'What does it take to make NGC grow?' The answer to my second question is that I need to not do everything. And sometimes it's my fault that I'm trying to do everything."

"Thank you, Matt. Allan?"

"One: How do I know I have enough money? I hear the two of them talking about plans for growth—even increasing wholesale acquisitions, which was not our original plan—and I think, 'Where are we getting the money to hire these people?' Two: I just need a little autonomy."

"Yes!" Reggie rubbed his hands together. "Just so you know, Allan, I hear that from pretty much every business that hits their plateau in resources. Now then, how about you, Charlotte?"

"Well. Honesty is mandatory, right?"

"It will help your brothers."

"Every night I ask myself, 'Should I go back there tomorrow?'"

"Really, Char?" Matt's face fell. "Honestly, I'm disappointed. But in myself. I want to know how we keep you here."

"I love you, Char," Allan grabbed his sister's hand.

"Do you ask yourself that, Allan?" Matt locked eyes with his brother. "I want to know."

Allan hemmed and hawed, tilting his head back and forth. "Not every night."

"Thanks for being honest." Matt frowned. "Sorry, Reggie, you're the one asking the questions."

"That's fine, Matt. Charlotte, you still owe us an answer to question 2."

"I want to be empowered. Not that I want to be over Matt—though I am over him in fixing toilets—but I think I can make a big difference here. I'm learning fast, and I see things before others see them. And I want to be empowered and recognized for it."

Reggie applauded. "Great answer. Great answer from everyone. Now…how are we going to do this? For the rest of today, we are going to do three things: make sure the right people are in the right seat, create a budget, and create a pro forma so Allan can know if he can hire people."

"That would make me happy." Allan raised his water bottle in a mock toast.

"Let's look at page 12," Reggie flipped in his workbook. "Succession planning. We are going to talk about the two positions I think you need to add right away."

"What's one of the positions?" Allan asked.

"Acquisitions," Matt answered.

"So under the 'Ops. Manager' example, write 'Acquisitions.'"

"You don't have to use names, but is there anyone in the building who could fill this position?"

"Barb has done a little work on it," Charlotte answered. "But I don't think that's her strength."

"From what I have heard you say today, I don't think you have the person in the building. Here's the next question. On a scale of 1 to 3, is the Acquisitions position an urgent need?"

"Three," Matt said. "And I see the other questions on the sheet. We definitely have poor internal benchmarks for acquisitions. Filling the seat would make a strong impact on our business. It requires a unique skill set of knowledge. I'd give a three to each of those. And I'd give a 2 for Low External Candidate Availability."

"This adds up to 14, which is over 10, so you need to add this position," Reggie said. "Before Allan worries, let me say that we will look at sales projections and if you can hire someone who will pay for himself."

"We would need someone who will work straight off of commissions, wouldn't we?" Charlotte asked.

Matt's eyes beamed like car headlights. He and Allan locked eyes.

"What are you thinking? You're scaring me," Allan said.

"Bob!" Matt's face lit up.

"That's what I thought you were thinking." Allan grimaced. "Bob Blackburn. Wow! That's a name I haven't heard in a long time."

"Who's Bob?" Charlotte asked. "I've got a bad feeling about this."

"He is a salesman from when we worked at Grant City Chevy." The thought of Bob taking his sales skills into real estate buoyed Matt. "He was legendary."

"Legendary?" Allan scoffed. "He was memorable. Legendary implies greatness. Bob was memorable for some questionable things."

"I'm sure he's matured in the last fifteen years," Matt said. "I can't believe I hadn't thought of this before."

"I'm skeptical," Allan offered.

"I'm not. I think it would be perfect."

"You can discuss who should fill the position after I leave," Reggie said. "For now, let's agree that we need the position."

"Agreed," Charlotte said with an exaggerated nod.

"The second position is Project Manager. How would you fill in the succession plan?"

Matt mulled over the chart. "My numbers come out to 12. Which is greater than 10. So we need to fill it."

"You get the picture," Reggie said. "There are some other positions to consider, but I think you start with these two. Before we talk about how to pay for it, we need to talk about talent optimization. So turn to page 14."

"Looks like a biology lesson!" Charlotte cheered.

"Heart, Head, Hands, and Feet," Reggie said. "Never thought of it as a biology lesson, but that's a way to present it, Charlotte. I might use that in future coaching. The measure of the heart is your desire. The 'heart' of an individual represents their inherent desire, their intrinsic motivation, and their passion. It is the driving force that propels them to stretch their capabilities and strive for peak performance. This desire, being a fundamental part of an individual's personality, determines how devoted they are to their role, their work, and by extension, the success of the organization."

"How do you really measure someone's heart?" Matt asked.

"Yours is three sizes too small," Charlotte joked.

"It might be," Matt said. "I'll wear that."

"That's a great question, Matt," Reggie said. "Measuring 'heart' can seem complex due to its subjective nature, but with the right tools, it's entirely feasible. You can get some insight into their values, aspirations, and passions through interviews, surveys, and just observing. Are they dedicated? Eager to shoulder responsibilities? Resilient in the face of challenges? Those seem like the characteristics of a person with a strong heart."

"Makes sense," Matt nodded.

"Heart is a desire assessment. The head is a behavioral assessment. What drives them? The 'head' is indicative of someone's behavioral traits and cognitive abilities. Behavioral traits can predict how a person is likely to act in different situations. Have you done any type of psychometric evaluations with employees?"

"No," Matt answered.

"Job performance observations?"

"Not really," Charlotte admitted.

"I have resources you can consider. There's a lot of ways you can help your employees grow in behavior and cognitive abilities."

"I'd like to do that," Matt said.

"Third component is the hands. This is a skills assessment for professional skills and experience."

"So, it's asking, 'What tangible skills do you bring to work?'" Allan asked.

"Yes. Where are they competent or qualified?"

"Can't I get that by looking at resumes or LinkedIn?" Matt asked.

"Yes! You should. You can also evaluate how they do on projects or see if they gravitate toward continuous learning and education. Do you offer any of that?"

Matt wrote on his notepad. "We will in the future!"

"Lastly, the feet are about upward mobility. Is there potential growth? This is dictated by their ambition, adaptability, and capacity to learn and evolve. Feet takes time to recognize. You need feedback from managers and colleagues and a work history to evaluate their potential for advancement." Reggie typed on his phone. "I'm sending you a link to an aptitude test. It will give you a taste of behavior and cognitive score. It will take you ten minutes. Let me know when you are done."

Matt went to work right away. He loved being tested and evaluated.

"I don't like this test," Allan said. "I worry this information will end up in the wrong hands."

"It's not like you're giving your bank account and social, Allan," Matt said.

"I could go either way on this test," Charlotte said. "Like Matt, I kind of want to know, but I also don't like being labeled."

"You like it, don't you, Matt?" Allan asked.

"Yes! I think I'm going to get answers I'm really happy with."

"And he wants everyone to see how awesome he is because of his results!" Charlotte said.

"Exactly! I'm not ashamed of that," Matt said.

When they were done with the assessment, Reggie accessed the results.

"Matt, you are a person looking for adventure and a man of high drive."

"Yes! That sounds like me. Let's go!"

"Charlotte, you are competitive. You also have drive, but not as much as Matt. You love to strategize."

"Wow!" Matt looked in awe at his sister. "You've always been competitive and strategizing. I've never thought of it in a good way."

Charlotte laughed. "I'm liking Reggie being here. There's a lot you haven't realized about me."

"Allan, your profile is no surprise," Reggie said. "You are formal. Your siblings are not. You are about precision. Matt doesn't care if he makes a mistake. You are introverted. And have zero desire to be in charge around others."

Allan beamed, "That is me."

"And Matt is impatient. Allan, you have moderate patience. Charlotte, I'm surprised that you have more patience than Allan."

Charlotte pumped her fist. "I was a girl with two older brothers. I had to have a little bit of patience."

"It looks like the three of you are in pretty good places. Allan, you are in a good seat, according to your profile. Matt needs to put you in a better position. Charlotte, you need a challenge, don't you?"

"Yes!"

"It's one thing for me to say that I think you are in a good position. But that's not my job as a coach to say. You are the one who has to work the job every day. So look at page 15. I'm going to ask you these questions. Matt, you go first. Does this position give you an emotional reward to do the job?"

"As a CEO, yes!" Matt paused. "But as a project manager or plumber? Absolutely not!"

Charlotte laughed. Sweat beaded on Allan's forehead.

"Okay, Allan," Reggie continued, "Does this position give you an emotional reward to do the job?"

Allan exhaled. "No. I'm frustrated. There's no accountability around spending. I can't make decisions on what's in the best interest of NGC. We just react to not having enough cash on hand. Bills pile up, and I can't pay them."

Matt bit his lip.

"If you bite any harder, you might draw blood, Matthew," Reggie said.

"Allan, don't you get a reward for rebuilding Grant City?" Matt asked.

"Are we?" Allan's question was pointed.

"Before you continue, Matt," Reggie interrupted, "you are asking the wrong question. Rebuilding NGC is a purpose and an inspiration. I'm asking if being the CFO gives Allan an emotional reward. Rebuilding NGC could inspire him in his CFO position or if he was a passive investor."

"Then I withdraw my question." Matt eyed Allan, observing his brother's gangly posture and how his eyes stared at his lap. "Sorry, Allan."

Reggie said, "Charlotte, you are next. Does your position give you an emotional reward to do the job?"

"Yes. When I can do it. I feel like it has allowed me to stand out," she answered.

"Tremendous! Here's the second question. Is this position high on your priority list?"

"Yes!" Matt said.

"Yes," Allan said.

"Absolutely," Charlotte answered.

"Question three. Do you produce quality work?"

Matt sneered. "No. I don't. I'd like to."

"Allan?"

"No. I can't because I don't have enough resources."

"What resources are you lacking?" Matt asked.

"Maybe cash on hand!" Allan threw his hands in the air.

"Makes sense," Matt said. "Sorry, Allan, I'm not trying to fight here. I'm trying to hear you out."

"I think I produce quality work," Charlotte answered.

"When I let you do your job?" Matt asked. "Were you going to add that?"

"You said it, not me!"

"Last question," Reggie said. "Do you get energy from this position?"

"Definitely!" Matt said.

Allan didn't answer. Before Matt could address the silence, Charlotte answered.

"Sometimes," Charlotte said, "and I like this job a lot when I am getting energy!"

Allan still didn't answer.

"Allan?" Reggie asked.

"No. But I'm not a high-energy person."

"Thank you, everyone, for honest answers. Look at page 17. Let's do a little skills assessment for your hands. Can you train someone else in your role?"

Matt said, "Maybe. I don't think anyone else can do it."

"What about your role as project manager or plumber?" Reggie asked.

"You have jokes now?"

"No. I'm serious. You need to get out of that role, but first, you need to train people."

"Then, yes. I can train someone else in those roles."

"Allan?"

"Yes. It would be easy to train someone in my role."

"Charlotte?"

"They'd need the right skill set, some creativity. But I can do it."

"The next question is this: have you worked in this sector or niche for 1 year or more?"

They each answered, "Yes."

"Question 3. Do you deliver results that achieve goals 90% of the time or more?"

Matt's eyes widened. "No. I have so many goals. I don't hit them."

"Yes," Allan said.

"If we had defined goals," Charlotte answered, "I'd say "yes."

"The last question," Reggie said, "is if you have more than one year of experience in this role. That's a 'yes' for all of you, correct?"

They all nodded.

"Then let's do a foot assessment, aka mobility assessment. First question. Are you willing to take on new challenges?"

"Of course!" Matt said.

"Not outside the realm of finance." Allan shook his head. "So I guess I have no feet."

"That's not what it means," Reggie said. "Allan, I sense you are frustrated with a lack of structure. Structure gives you great comfort."

"It does!"

"We are creating structure here. If NGC implements this coaching, I think you're going to find a lot of satisfaction," Reggie said. "Charlotte, how about you?"

"I am definitely willing to take on new challenges!"

"Question 2. Are you willing to learn and improve?"

They all answered "yes."

"Question 3. Are you willing to communicate?

They all answered "yes."

"Last one. Are you willing to be a critical thinker and problem solver?

"Yes!" Matt answered.

"Definitely!" Charlotte said.

"Allan, what's your answer?" Reggie asked.

"Yes!" Allan answered. "I love doing those things! I'm at my happiest when I can do them!"

"Then, Allan, I would definitely say that you have mobility and 'feet!'"

"I'll feel like a whole person with feet, hands, a heart, and head when I can actually have a budget and be accountable for the finances."

"That's a great point, Allan!" Reggie observed. "We still need to talk about Talent Development, spending money on it, and creating a pro forma. Let's break!"

CHAPTER 14

The Resource Wrap-Up

"Let's wrap this up for today!" Reggie stood in the conference room doorway and waved the siblings over.

"I'm not going to lie. That last session with the pro forma formation was rough," Matt said.

"I loved it!" Allan countered.

"That's why you are the CFO!" Matt said. "And I don't want to be in that seat. It's all yours."

Once everyone was seated at the table, Reggie said, "You didn't hire me as a coach just to point out everything you have been doing wrong. Before I leave today, we need to review what you must do to start immediate improvements."

Matt's fingers hovered over his keyboard. "I'm ready."

"I have four goals for you. The first is that you need to start tracking weekly numbers. Matt, who will do that?"

"I'd like to do that!" Allan said.

"Then Allan will do it, Reggie," Matt answered.

"Great. Second, you need to run a weekly meeting. It will be bumpy and clumsy, but you start somewhere."

"What do we do in this meeting?" Charlotte asked.

"Review the numbers. Next time we meet, I will teach you different meetings and their frequencies, but for now, you need to establish the meeting by reviewing the numbers and seeing where you are at on a weekly basis."

"What's number three?" Matt asked.

"Hire someone in acquisitions. Maybe promote someone to project manager."

"Hire Bob! Check!" Matt looked at his siblings' reactions.

Allan scrunched his face. Charlotte looked back and forth between her brothers, seemingly unsure of what to make of hiring Bob.

"And the fourth," Reggie said, "is using the pro forma we just created and building a budget."

"Yes!" Allan pumped his fist. "A budget."

"A budget that has money to pay Bob!" Matt raised his eyebrows towards Allan.

Allan folded his arms and leaned back. "If we want to get someone in here right away, he might work."

"Hiring Bob will be up to you three. Get those four tasks accomplished, and then we will meet for Inspiration Day and Systems Day back-to-back."

Matt walked Reggie out to the rental car. "I can't thank you enough for coming today."

Reggie looked Matt square in the eyes. "You can do this. Charlotte is a great resource. She is learning, but you can mold her."

Allan poked his head out the front door. "I will have a budget! Thank you, Reggie!"

"He seems inspired! Thank you."

"You're welcome. I'd keep an eye on Allan."

"Can you explain?"

"I think he's considering leaving."

"Allan? No way."

"There are signs. I'm not saying that he will, but I think there's something missing for him. We'll learn more next time when I come for Inspiration Day and Systems Day."

"What stood out to you today with Allan?"

"His commitment to the seat. His frustration. He doesn't sound frustrated, but he uses words that are frustrating." Reggie put his satchel in the back seat and closed the rental car's door. "I really do think that the structure we talked about today will help Allan settle into his role. You need to do this if you want to keep your brother."

"Okay. But I still can't imagine him leaving."

"Just keep him inspired!"

"How?" Matt asked.

Reggie opened the driver's door. "I'll tell you on Inspiration Day!"

CHAPTER 15

The Weekly Meeting

"I have never been this excited to come to a weekly meeting!" Matt charged into the conference room. "Bob's been killing it in acquisitions. I can't wait to see the numbers, Allan! I can't wait to show Reggie next week when he comes!"

Allan remained silent as he navigated to the spreadsheet. His lips were tight.

Charlotte's contorted looked painful. She stared at the floor.

"Are the numbers not good? I thought that Bob—"

"Bob is what's not good, Matt!" Charlotte's glare was fueled by anger.

Matt looked at the numbers that Allan cast to the TV. "That's more revenue than the first ten weeks of the year! The numbers from our three-month plan have been blown up by Bob! Are you jealous?"

Charlotte seethed as she sucked air through her teeth. About to speak, she held up a finger and slowly exhaled.

"What is going on?" Matt looked back and forth between Charlotte's stabbing stare and Allan, who stared at his keyboard.

No one spoke.

"This isn't about money?" Matt held his hands out. "Guys, I need help here. There's something I don't know, and I need you to tell me.

Honestly, the last two minutes are making me angry, and I don't want to be. What's going on?"

"Bob is blowing up sales, but he's also blowing up the staff and the chemistry." Charlotte struggled to get the words out in a regular cadence, interrupted by pushing back her tears and emotions.

Matt reached for the tissue box.

"I don't want a tissue!" Her voice suddenly carried the anger she had shown moments earlier. "I want Bob gone."

Matt's jaw dropped. "What?"

"You haven't noticed, Matt?" Allan motioned towards the door. "They hate him out there."

Matt sat in silence, thinking through interactions with Bob. "He's been a nice person and great at acquisitions."

Through the open conference room door, Matt heard someone yell, "Bob just got out of his car!"

An office door slammed. Through the open blinds of the conference room, Matt could see the cubicle employees get up and head for the breakroom or bathroom.

"Perfect timing." Charlotte's smile twisted on her lips. "You've really never noticed."

"I'm feeling a little foolish at this moment. I hadn't noticed that people avoided him."

"He's coming!" Charlotte spun her chair towards the TV.

Allan feverishly typed with his head down. "Char, we can reanalyze the metrics after this meeting and–"

"Talking about our rock star weekly numbers?" Bob Blackburn stuck his shiny bald head into the conference room.

Matt had found Bob uplifting, but today he tried to examine his acquisitions guy from the viewpoint of the others.

Without invitation, Bob walked into the meeting. "Matt, we are rock stars. Your vision is killing it! And Charlotte—your little sister—she is a rock star in the making. She's an opening act right now. But someday, little sister is going to be a rockstar in this business!"

"Rockstar? I'd like to throw a rock at your head so you'd see stars."

Bob's frown even made his triple chin look like it was sad. "Oh? Did I do something? Sorry, Matt. I'm not sure what it was, but I'm sorry that she's upset."

Matt stood. "I'll handle it, Bob! Can you close the door on your way out?"

Bob continued further into the conference room and put his arm around Matt. "Let me know what I can do to help little Charlotte. Goodbye, Allan. Charlotte." Bob left and closed the door.

"Okay. Looking at that through the lens of this morning's conversation was eye-opening," Matt admitted.

"What did it open your eyes to, Matt?" Charlotte bent a pen with her hands.

"Ummm…you're going to splatter ink on yourself." Matt rolled his chair next to Charlotte's and took the pen from her. He placed it on the table and held her hand. "I see how his word choices can be demeaning."

"He said that he was sorry that Charlotte was upset, not that he was sorry he had done anything wrong," Allan said.

"That wasn't empathetic at all," Matt agreed. "But–"

Charlotte's head shot up. "There should be no 'but's here."

"But can we start having a conversation with him before we fire him?"

No one answered.

"Give him more chances? Our systems are non-existent. We might need to first iron out what our employee policies are and hold him to those?"

"How long will that take?" Charlotte's question was sharp and suspicious.

"I can talk to him today. Policies…sheesh…I'm not sure. I think Reggie will tell us next week. But I can give him a verbal warning."

Allan nodded. "I can't speak for Charlotte, but I can agree to that for now. I know you, Matt, and I know you don't back down to anyone. I believe you'll have a frank and stern conversation with Bob."

"Thank you, Allan. Charlotte?"

"Talk to him right now before anyone else has to interact with him today."

"Let's postpone this meeting. And Char…." Matt waited for her to look at him. "I'm sorry that I didn't notice any of this."

Charlotte stood and hugged Matt. "That's okay. I figured he acts differently around you. It's just the rest of us are tired of the way he acts around us."

Allan's long wingspan embraced them both. "I couldn't miss out on this family moment."

Matt laughed and pushed him away. "Feelings overload. Back to business! Let's reconvene after lunch."

They reconvened the weekly meeting immediately after lunch.

"How did the talk with Bob go?" Allan asked.

"He heard me. He respects me."

"Did you make any ultimatums?" Charlotte asked.

"I told him that unkindness will cost him his job."

"That's kind of vague." Charlotte protested.

"What else do you want?" Matt snapped.

Charlotte held her hands up in surrender.

"Ease off of her, Matt." Allan's voice remained soft and calm. "I know you like the numbers this week, but sometimes there's more than that."

Matt raised his voice. "Of course, there's more than that, Allan. We're revitalizing Grant City."

"Hopefully."

"Hopefully?"

Allan shrugged. "Seems like we are moving further and further away from our purpose. Where there is no vision, the people perish. You know Dad would quote that. What's the vision, Matt? Putting up with Bob because he makes big bucks?"

Matt seethed. He pushed his chair away from the conference room table. "Let's have this meeting tomorrow."

CHAPTER 16

The Leadership Assessment

Matt grew tired of pacing, so he sat on a bench outside of the NGC offices. He looked at his text from Reggie.

"Be there in five. - Reggie."

Matt swiped left. The text came in at 7:52. It was only 7:55, but it felt like Reggie was late. Matt didn't want to go back into the office. The cool spring morning was still warmer than recent mornings. Besides, the atmosphere in the office felt like a hot and heavy humid day. Sitting outside was a relief.

Last week's talk with Bob went well in the moment. No one had spoken up against Bob since, but there was an uneasiness in the office, like the silent tension of an impending quick draw in a Western movie. Matt knew someone was about to fire a shot. He just hoped it wasn't while Reggie was with them these next two days.

Reggie's rental car pulled into the parking lot. Reggie stepped out of his car and said, "You ready for two days? Inspiration and Systems! Let's go."

"I'm ready." Matt gestured to the front door. "Can we go to my office before we begin?"

"Of course."

Matt closed his office door. "Things are tense here."

"No way." Reggie playfully gasped and put his hands over his mouth. "Let me guess; people are asking you how to do everything all the time?"

"Yes!"

"You are making some money these last few months, and new problems have popped up between people's personalities and spirits?"

"Yes."

"And you thought everyone would be happy by now?"

"Exactly!"

"And you thought wrong, Matthew. Things are changing. Equilibrium has been disrupted. People will leave. New people will come. Today is going to be a great day. We are going to talk about inspiration."

"Can I tell you what's going on?"

"No. Let today play out, and let's see what is revealed. Let's get to it!"

Reggie and Matt entered the conference room.

Charlotte hugged Reggie. "I'm happy you're here. Need anything?" Charlotte pointed to the coffee bar.

"Not right now, but thank you! Hi Allan!" Reggie craned his neck back and looked up at Allan. "How's the weather up there?"

Allan thought a moment. "I have no funny response for you."

"That's okay. You just be good with the numbers and don't worry about comedy. Let's get started."

Reggie hit a few keys on his laptop, and a RISE graphic mirrored onto the TV.

"As always, let's talk about good news. Matt, what's good?"

"Sales! We have succeeded and paid back loans to Allan. And working with my siblings is good."

"Charlotte, what's good?" Reggie asked.

"Many numbers are good."

"Do you want to expand on that?"

"No."

"Okay," Reggie said. "What's good, Allan?"

"I wasn't thinking this until Matt said it, but they paid back my loan. I've had more autonomy as the CFO. Matt's done a good job with that. I think getting us to think in terms of seats has been really helpful."

"You ready to talk about Inspiration?"

"Yes!" Matt said.

No one else answered.

"Inspiration is about Leadership, Long-Term Vision, Culture and Short-Term Vision. At NGC, the times are changing. You're getting leaner and stronger. This can upset the status quo. That's why we start with leadership. You have to lead them through the changes. Charlotte, are you a leader here?"

Charlotte straightened up as though the question caught her off guard. "Ummm…Absolutely."

"Allan, are you a leader here?"

Allan pulled his lips tight and paused, slowly letting out a "Yes."

"Matt, are you a leader here?"

"Yes!"

"Alright then. Let's start with the importance of leadership. If you aren't convinced, I will convince you in the next few moments. Look at page 31 in the curriculum."

An orange and black graphic appeared on the TV showing four elements of leadership with "Encourage" in the center of them.

"If you are going to lead people, you need to challenge them. This means you challenge the status quo and take a proactive approach to identify and address problems, improve processes, and create new solutions. How's that going here?" Reggie chuckled.

Allan said, "Address problems and create new solutions? We've created new problems."

Matt noticed Charlotte and Allan scrutinizing his reaction. "We have created new problems," he admitted.

"Hopefully, we will address some of them today. Let's move on to the second point. As a leader, you need to inspire. You need a vision. We'll talk about that today. You need to create one. Do you have ambitious goals that will inspire and motivate your team and move them towards success?"

Allan raised his hand. "Is that a rhetorical question? Because if it isn't, I'd have to say that none of that is clearly defined."

"It was rhetorical," Reggie said. "The answer is usually 'no.' Businesses often need Inspiration Day because vision and goals are not in place."

"Well, it's good to know that we suck like everyone else." Matt looked to his siblings for a response.

Charlotte raised her eyebrows and nodded. "I don't want to suck like everyone else, but we can own that for right now."

"Third is empower. Are you empowering others?"

Charlotte and Allan simultaneously looked at Matt.

Matt threw up his hands in surrender. "I think that was a rhetorical question again."

Reggie continued as though there hadn't been an interruption. "Empower your followers. It develops a culture of collaboration and trust. Foster an environment of shared responsibility. Model good business behavior. It sets an example that employees and colleagues can follow. It fosters a culture of success."

Reggie cleared his throat and looked at each one of them. "If you are the leaders, you need to be encouragers. Encourage the people out there and encourage each other. Encouragement motivates. Encouragement makes them engaged. Encouragement empowers. Encourage them to act. It will set the proper tone for the work environment.

"So here's what we are going to do. You're going to turn to page 32 and complete the leadership assessment. Then, you add up your score. Then we will discuss them."

Matt scanned the leadership assessment. His impulse was to give himself good scores. Judging by the moods of his siblings lately, he knew he was failing somewhere in leadership. A question about conflict management stood out to him. He knew he was failing at it. This had to be an honest assessment for the sake of Allan and Charlotte.

Reggie returned to the conference room after ten minutes. "That should have been enough time to complete the assessment. Matt, what's your score?"

"50"

"Allan?"

"38"

"Charlotte?"

Charlotte's eyes grew wider than the grin that was already on her face. "51!" She pumped her fist.

Matt protested. "This isn't a contest. It's not like you won. I mean, you graded yourself."

"You've always hated losing," Allan added.

"I didn't lose. She graded herself. Let me grade her."

"Oh, please! Let me grade you, Matt. We'll see if you get a 50."

"I always love coaching families," Reggie said. "Let's get down to business. Allan, your score is lower than theirs. What are some of the areas you need improvement in?"

"Which ones did I score a one?"

"Yes."

Allan counted down the list. "Eight of them. You want all of them?"

"No. Just give me a couple of reasons why you gave yourself a one."

"I have found that I don't love innovating on the fly. That's needed for a business that still struggles with resources. I have the ability to lead in a more stable setting. Secondly, one question that stood out to me is the one about being the face. That's not my desire at all."

"Thank you, Allan. We'll come back to this on the next assessment. Charlotte, where did you score low?"

"I gave myself a single one. It was aligned with the statement, 'I feel as a leader, I am instrumental in developing new leaders to play an important role in the future of the company.' We're trying to get our act together here, and developing new leaders isn't happening."

Reggie raised his eyebrows. "Why not?"

"I don't think we think about it. I think all three of us are trying to figure out how we should lead individually."

"I'm sure we'll come back to that, too. Matt, how about you?"

"I gave myself three ones. I'd like to talk about each of them. First, I don't embrace using conflict management to unite team members. We have some conflict in-house that has been dividing us."

"What else?"

"Same as Char. We're not developing new leaders. Third, I don't have the ability to respond effectively to the most sensitive inquiries or complaints. I would have answered this differently two weeks ago because I thought I knew how to do this, but the last two weeks have shown that I don't know how to do it or even recognize where to apply it."

Reggie stood and walked to the TV and felt along the side and underneath for the power button. "There it is." Reggie pressed it, and the screen went blank.

"Let's pause a moment. I'm sensing something in the room. It feels bad, but it will be good for the long term. I sense frustration from unresolved issues. I feel the tension between you three. However, it's different from many other rooms I've been in. I think the three of you want to figure it out. I don't think anyone is lying. I don't think anyone is pretending. I don't think there is pride."

"Other than Charlotte bragging about outscoring Matt!" Allan patted himself on the back for his joke as they all laughed.

Reggie pointed at Allan. "See what I'm saying. There is no bitterness between you. You can make jokes and laugh. I can work with that. We can work through this."

"So what's next?" Matt asked.

"The management assessment on page 33."

The siblings jumped into the assessment. Matt analyzed the questions, constantly wondering if he graded himself too leniently. Then he wondered what Charlotte graded herself for some of the questions. He did the quick math in his head and decided that he should come out ahead in this one.

"Let's call this meeting to order!" Reggie grinned as he pounded the table like a judge. "Would you like to go first this time, Matt?" Reggie asked.

"I'd like to go last again."

"You are the boss. Let's start with Charlotte, then. Tell me what you scored, and then tell me a positive and a negative."

"This time, I'm not concerned if I won." Charlotte scanned her page. "I gave myself a 44."

"Forty-four?" The words sprayed from Matt's mouth.

"I take it you didn't score that high," Charlotte said. "I gave myself two ones. The core value questions aren't defined. I feel that we're breaking them, but nothing is set in stone."

"What's the other one?"

"That I thrive in effectively integrating all major functions of the organization. I'd like to do it. But we're not doing it, so I'm not thriving at it."

"What's positive?"

Her eyes brightened. "I gave myself a lot of twos. Overall, I love what I do. I saw myself decorating houses, not buying and selling them. But I love helping our employees reach their potential. I enjoy it when things are a little messy, and we can solve some problems. Except for a few things, I enjoy leading. I'm finding that I am a leader and wouldn't have called myself before a few months ago. I am finding a lot of satisfaction with having responsibility."

Reggie pumped his fist. "Yes! That is exciting. You are an incredible resource to this company. And you know it. Allan, how about you?"

Allan counted down the list. "Charlotte beat me by a touchdown and a two-point conversion. I totaled 36. I gave myself ten ones. I guess I don't think of myself as a manager of others. I manage myself well."

"Tell me a couple of reasons why you gave yourself those ones."

"That's easy. I don't like leading. I don't really like conflict. I don't like people looking to me for direction unless I'm certain of what I'm doing. And—" Allan pointed at Matt. "—Don't get mad. We don't have procedures and core values laid out, so I gave myself a one on those because we've failed to deliver them."

Reggie's face twisted. "Are you punishing yourself?"

Allan bit his finger. "Probably."

"But are those your fault?"

"Yes. I'm a leader here. They are not done. We're in year three."

"Okay. I think you are being a little hard on yourself. But let's see what we learn from Matt."

"I fall between Allan and Charlotte. I gave myself a 38."

"That's way too low," Charlotte protested.

"No. Allan is right about results. I consider myself a leader. It's part of my personality. But when we look at the current situation, we certainly don't see structured management, and the lack of it has hurt us."

"Where did you score well?" Reggie asked.

"Questions about accountability. I'm not afraid of it. I embrace it. I scored '3s' on questions about vision and the future. But I've missed seeing some problems around here. What good is planning the future if you'll be dead from cancer?"

"This conversation is healthy," Reggie said. "Let's come back to this in a little while. It sounds like there's a values clash in leadership. It also sounds like Charlotte and Allan aren't talking too much about it, but Matt, you're emoting about it. We'll figure this out."

CHAPTER 17

The Leadership Audit

"Good afternoon!" Reggie patted his belly. "It's time to get back to work. We're on page 35. This is my favorite content in the RISE process. We have a little more work to do on leadership, but then we will talk a lot about core values. It draws some lines in the sand. Sometimes, people quit during this time. Everyone who remains is galvanized. This is going to be a pivotal afternoon in the history of your business."

Reggie made eye contact with each person. "Make anyone nervous?"

Allan raised his hand. "Right here."

"Would you tell us why?"

"I'm afraid of what we will find. The biggest reason I'm here is because of this family." Allan pointed to his siblings. "And I personally struggle because sometimes this family keeps me from Lisa and Theodore and Harriet."

Reggie sympathetically nodded. "Breakups happen, Allan. People need to be true to their core values, which sometimes means walking away. Though it's painful in the moment, it's usually the best for everyone."

Allan's sad smile disappeared as he looked at the questions. "I don't want to go first."

"I'll gladly start," Matt said.

"Brave man!" Reggie said. "What are the biggest challenges you faced as a leader this week?"

"The last week has been very different. I'm in a better place than I was on your first visit. But the Bob debacle has driven a wedge between me and Charlotte. And when I walk into the office, I feel like everyone is shaking their head at me."

"The Bob debacle?"

"May I?" Allan sarcastically raised his hand. "It's just better that I tell the story since I'm not one of the two parties. When you were here last time, we decided to hire someone in acquisitions who would get paid on commissions. We hired Bob."

"We used to work with Bob," Matt interjected.

"Yes. At Grant City Chevy. I had a job there throughout college. Matt had a summer job there when he was in college. Matt and Bob hit it off because they're both…." Allan rubbed his chin.

"Both what?" Matt asked suspiciously.

"You are both extroverts with big personalities who talk big." Allan turned to his brother. "You have toned down somewhat——Bob has not."

Matt nodded. "That's fair."

"When we worked with Bob at the dealership, he was the king of sales. He could seal the deal. But he rubbed a lot of people the wrong way. It got to this point where people would say, 'He thinks he's God!'"

Matt laughed. "And then people started saying, 'Oh my Bob!' when they were annoyed."

"They did," Allan agreed. "But Bob caught wind of it."

"Did he get mad?" Reggie asked.

"No," Allan answered. "He liked it. He started saying, 'Oh my Bob!' And then when he heard someone else say it, do you know what he said?"

Reggie shook his head. "No idea."

"He said, 'You shall not take the Bob's name in vain.'"

Reggie put his hand on his mouth and slowly shook his head. "He did not."

"He did."

Reggie smirked at Matt. "And this is the guy you hired?"

Matt threw his hands in the air. "Yes. It's been a financial success."

"You've sat there pretty silent, Charlotte. Anything to say?"

"Not right now," she answered. "I might say it with the wrong spirit."

"Okay. So…Charlotte, what are the biggest challenges you faced as a leader this week?"

"Keeping up the spirit around here because of Bob. I'm not a cheerleader like Matt. I've had a hard time because the Bob problem is personal. It's not a problem, like we can't pay a bill. It feels like an attack on me."

Reggie empathetically groaned. "Thank you for sharing that and for being honest about your limitations and hurt. Your turn, Allan."

Allan folded his hands together. "My biggest challenge has been keeping focused on the finances instead of getting dragged into the Bob debacle conversations."

Reggie said, "Thanks! Question 2. Matt, how would you characterize your leadership over the past week?"

"Realistic. I've done what I need to do to keep deals happening and getting us to the point where we can improve Grant City."

"Charlotte?"

"Team oriented. There have been some people who feel Matt has let them down by not firing Bob already. Though I don't like Bob, I've deflected the negativity aimed at Matt. But I do have some negativity of my own."

"Understood. I think we'll be able to sort some of this out this afternoon. Allan, what's your answer?"

"I just try to lead myself and my assistant. She doesn't like Bob. But she's a sweetheart and worries about what will happen to Bob if we fire him. We keep plugging along in our finance niche. As far as numbers go, I've done the job leading. As far as people go, I'm kind of avoiding the whole Bob situation."

"Third question," Reggie said. "What strategies have proven most effective in motivating and inspiring your team over the past week?"

Matt, Charlotte, and Allan looked back and forth at each other. Charlotte's face broke first, and they all started laughing.

Matt said, "Can I tell you something I did three weeks ago? Because my this-isn't-a-big-deal strategy with Bob isn't working.

"My strategy," Charlotte said, "is to galvanize around our hatred of Bob. I'm not going to lie. I've used it."

"Is ignoring a problem considered a strategy?" Allan asked.

"That question went as well as I thought it would," Reggie joked. "Last question. What core values did you promote in the workplace this week?"

"Ooh!" Matt exclaimed. "Accomplishment. Building Grant City."

"But you've avoided others." Charlotte's snarky answer got under Matt's skin. "I've promoted decency towards humanity."

"I think I've promoted determination and getting the job done with all the distractions around us," Matt retorted.

Charlotte's eyes were ravenous. "Well, then, Reggie, I promoted the core value of putting up with indecent humanity and clueless owners!"

"That's not a core value!" Matt objected. "Reggie, tell her that's not a core value! If she valued it, she wouldn't be mad about doing it."

Charlotte seethed at Matt. She pushed back from the table, smacked her pen onto the table, and walked out.

Allan stood. "I'm going to go promote the core value of hiding in my office." He left.

"Thanks for not telling Allan that hiding in your office isn't a core value, Matt." Reggie plopped into his leather chair and sighed. "What's your next move?"

Matt sucked his cheeks in, biting the insides of them. "I need to apologize." Matt rose from his chair and knocked on Charlotte's office door. She didn't answer.

"You okay, Matt?" Bob's question startled Matt. Bob motioned to Charlotte's office. "She'll learn soon enough how businesses really work. You're doing a great job of toughening her up."

Matt winced like he had a migraine. "I need you to stay out of this right now, Bob."

"I know how it is working with women."

Matt imagined spinning Bob around and kicking him in the butt.

Bob read Matt's face. "I'm working on four new leads from this morning. It's going to be a good week." He winked and walked away.

"Char!" Matt knocked. "I'm sorry. Can we talk?"

"I'm not in there."

Matt wheeled around and saw Charlotte down the hallway, exiting the ladies' room.

"Did you think I was going to lock myself in my office and cry like a girl?"

"Is the timing bad to make a joke and say that is what Bob thought?"

Charlotte pursed her lips. "Probably." She smiled. "Listen, Matt. I'm not sure if you owe me an apology, but I owe you one. I'm sorry that I didn't put away my feelings and walked into Inspiration Day with a chip on my shoulder."

Matt vehemently shook his head. "No. Do not apologize for your feelings. I am sorry for trying to win an irrelevant argument."

"No. I am sorry for outscoring you on the management surveys." Charlotte looked up and started laughing.

Matt laughed, too. "I forgive you for inflating your scores."

"I forgive you for hiring Bob."

"But his numbers are so good!"

Charlotte tilted her head towards the conference room. "Let's get back in there."

"I first need to extract Allan, who locked himself in his office and is probably crying."

CHAPTER 18

The Core Values

"Look at page 37," Reggie said. "There's an exercise you need to write out. You're going to identify Core Values, and we're going to use those to determine the Core Values of NGC Properties. The goals and objectives of your company must remain in harmony with its core values. You must incorporate these principles, beliefs, and ideals into organizational decision-making processes. This sustains ethical and moral standards.

"Ethical and moral. So other than making money?" Allan asked.

"Making money could be a value," Reggie answered. "Whatever the core value, the employees need to be aligned. They then have a better understanding of expectations and how their work contributes to overall success. If they align with core values, you will have a positive workplace environment through trust, respect, collaboration, and shared goals."

Matt scowled as Allan and Char peeked up from their books. Charlotte silently mouthed, "Positive workplace environment," and smirked at him.

"I'll give you fifteen minutes to do step one," Reggie said. "You need to internalize. List the three most impactful people in your life. Then select the four words that describe what you most appreciate about them."

Matt sighed. Thinking about the past was painful. Some memories were painful, but most of the pain came from thinking back on events he could no longer do anything about. He wanted to move on to thinking about the future.

"Do we have to finish this today?" Matt asked.

Reggie chuckled. "Yes. It's crucial to the rest of the day. And crucial to clarifying some of the issues we've come across."

Matt grimaced.

"I love doing this!" Charlotte looked up from her workbook with teary eyes. "It allows me to honor people to whom honor is due."

Matt tapped his pen on the workbook.

Allan looked up. "A little less noise?"

"Sorry." Matt dropped his pen and reclined in the office chair.

"Writer's block?" Reggie asked.

"No," Allan huffed. "Matt's having emotional resistance."

Charlotte snorted. "Ask Reggie to coach you through it."

Reggie held out his arms like he was looking to hug someone. "That's why I'm here."

"So, I'm listing three people who have inspired me?" Matt asked.

"Impacted you," Reggie answered.

"Impacted me. Then, I pick words. What do the words do?"

"Did you read the instructions?" Charlotte interjected.

Allan laughed. "'What do the words do?' Words explain what you are thinking or feeling. To be honest, Matt. I'm enjoying this. You've always been the one who picks up quickly how to do things."

Charlotte loudly whispered to Allan, "I'm enjoying it, too."

"Isn't it tough to work with your siblings, Matt?" Reggie asked. "Who are people who have impacted you, and what did you appreciate about them? Who is someone you're considering?"

Matt answered, "My dad and mom."

"What do you appreciate about them?"

Matt pushed his chair from the table. "I really don't like going there." He shook his head. "Just...can't right now."

Reggie's voice softened. "I'm sorry, Matt. I don't want to push that. Is there someone else?"

"Juan Perez. I met him in Chicago, right outside my apartment building. He was helping a homeless person. He was in the neighborhood because he was rehabbing an apartment building near mine. We struck up a conversation and then a friendship. He believed he could make a difference. I wasn't making a difference in my corporate job, but I wanted to. He helped me believe I could do this."

"Maybe you should write down 'belief.'" Reggie pointed to the workbook.

"Okay." Matt wrote it down.

"Tell me more about Juan."

"He told me how he had managed a UPS facility near the loop. He had four kids and a wife to care for, but he left the good and steady salary and incredible health insurance for the chance at freedom and a chance for his kids to never have to work a job like he worked. Man, he was daring."

"So maybe you should write down 'daring.'"

"Makes sense. Some Saturdays, we would go to lunch. He always had his eyes open for two things. The first was potential buildings to buy. People would be moving stuff in or out of a place, and he'd walk in like he lived there and start talking to the people about what was going on. No one ever told him to get out. He just always was looking for a deal, to get one step closer to his goal."

"So he had drive?"

"Yes! He had drive. I admire his drive."

"What was the other thing he had his eyes open to?"

"Homeless people. They weren't hard to find. He always had a roll of bills for them. He'd even buy some meals in to-go containers and hand them out."

"You admired his generosity?"

"Yes."

"Sounds like you have belief, daring, drive, and generous."

Matt beamed with pride. "I like that. That's what I like about Juan."

"Who else?"

"I'm not just saying this. Allan needs to be on my list."

Charlotte's head popped up. "He's on my list, too."

Allan muttered, "Don't get your hopes up; neither of you are on my list."

"Can I say what I admire about Allan?" Charlotte asked.

"Let Matt go first so your answers don't influence him," Reggie said.

"Allan is…," Matt paused for effect. "He is a teacher. I've always admired that about him. He would help me with school. He helped Char with school. I remember when we worked at the dealership, and Allan would be so patient, showing older people how to use the technology. He's willing to stop and explain."

"What did you write down?" Reggie asked.

"Teacher. Then, he has integrity. I've seen it this week. I've seen it all my life. And then…." Matt trailed off. He cleared his throat. "When…ummm…dad and mom passed, there were two things about him that I'll always remember. He just had faith in God. He had a belief that, somehow, this would be okay. It was so crappy because Charlotte was almost in junior high. But Allan believed it would be okay, and he did everything he could to make it okay. He and Lisa were young and married, and they took in Charlotte. I was finishing up college and had my job in Chicago. I was going to come back and help, but Allan pulled me aside and said that I didn't have to give up my dream at the moment. He said that he and Lisa were already living their dream and that they would be okay, and they could take care of Charlotte."

Matt wiped the tears from his eyes, expecting Charlotte to mock him. She had tears coming down her own eyes and watched with an admiring smile.

"Reggie," Matt continued, "Allan just filled in for dad. Dad was generous. He had integrity. He was a man of faith. I'm not a religious person to the level of my dad, but he loved God, and he loved the Bible, and he saw his life as building something for God. It gave him drive. It gave him belief. He cared so much for his family. He cared so much for others."

"I had dad, too," Allan said. "He and Mom died in a car accident. They would give time to Celebrate Recovery at their church. One night, on the way home, they were hit by a drug addict who was high. Head-on collision."

"I'm so sorry," Reggie stepped over between Allan and Charlotte and embraced their shoulders. "They were impactful people. Sounds like they did a lot for other people."

"I'd like to share mine," Charlotte said.

"Go for it," Reggie answered.

"First was Dad. I put love and respect for others. Integrity. Faith. Desire. I put Mom second."

"I had Mom on my list, too!" Allan said.

"For Mom, I put integrity. Faith and family. Love and respect for others. Teacher."

"Mom was a teacher," Matt said. "She insisted on teaching me to be a man who wouldn't expect his wife to do all the laundry and cooking."

"Did it work?" Reggie asked.

"I can sort laundry. Pair socks. Order DoorDash. That way, there are no dishes for Jean to clean up. That's about it."

"For Jean to clean up?" Charlotte pried. "Why isn't that your job, too?"

Matt scowled. "Just tell us what you admire about your third person, Charlotte."

Charlotte smirked like she knew she'd won the moment. "Allan has integrity. Belief and faith. He's more devoted to faith than Matt and I. He's devoted to family and others. I hope my husband is as devoted as Allan. He's just always looking out for others. He's a teacher. I added a fifth one: persistence/tenacity."

"Nice!" Reggie's smile turned into a frown as he thought. "Allan, it sounds like you are the glue at NGC."

Allan stared at his lap and scrunched into a contorted posture. "No. Matt is. Char is becoming it, too. I don't have the energy to be the glue like they do."

"Glue doesn't have energy," Matt objected. "It just gets gloopy and dry and crusty."

Charlotte laughed. "You kind of killed Reggie's compliment there."

"But it has to do that to hold things together." Matt chuckled, "Allan, you understand I'm not insulting you, right?"

"Yes." Allan still looked uncomfortable.

Matt scrunched his face at Charlotte. "Such an instigator."

"Allan, will you share your three?" Reggie asked.

"Yes. Yes." Allan snapped out of his trance.

"Dad: Sacrifice for others and generous. Integrity. Faith. Drive. Family.

Mom: Integrity. Nurturing. Love and Respect for Others. Time for Others. Generous.

Mr. Miller, my HS accounting teacher: Inspirational. Professional. Intelligent. He cared for students and made them feel like family. Generous with time."

"Thank you, Allan," Reggie said. "Now turn to page 39. I want you to group all the words from your three people into no more than four groupings. For instance, I heard the word "integrity" a lot. I also heard words like "sacrifice" and "others" that can be grouped together. "Belief" and "faith" could be grouped together, but for some people, those might have different meanings. Then, step three is to visualize and come up with one word for the group.

"Can I ask a dumb question?" Matt waved at Reggie.

"Only if it's truly dumb," Reggie dryly answered.

"You want us to lump this into four groups. I have generous giver, family, others, and teacher. To me, those all fall under the same category. Is that too broad?"

"What category would you put them under?"

"Generosity."

"Family is under generosity?"

"Is that wrong?" Matt asked as though he questioned himself.

"It's not right or wrong. I'm trying to draw out why you would group those together. I suspect Allan would group them separately."

"I would," Allan said. "I'm a little intimidated by how much you notice, Reggie."

Reggie grinned. "I am an expert coach for a reason."

"I would group them together because...," Matt bit on his pen. "Giving to others is generous. Juan giving money to a homeless person is generous. Allan giving the space to me, and Charlotte is generous. When I think of Mom and family, she was always giving and generous. So generous seems like an umbrella over all of those."

"That makes sense," Reggie said.

"I disagree," Allan said.

"You don't have to agree," Reggie said. "In fact, it's very important that you each retain your integrity as you do this. Your answers need to be your answers. They are your core values and not anyone else's."

"Okay. I have four," Matt sang. "In order they are Drive, Generosity, Integrity, Belief."

"Mine are almost the same. Different order," Charlotte said. "Respect. Drive. Integrity. Belief. Generosity."

"So, I'm more generous than you because it's higher on my list?"

"Well," she cocked her head to the side, "I noticed that you don't even have respect on your list. But I could have told you that before we started."

"Well, if I had actually restricted myself to four like Reggie said, then maybe I would have it on my list."

"Like it would have been."

"You'll never know because I followed the rules."

"That's a first!"

"Whoa!" Reggie held up his hands. "Bell rang. Go back to your corners. The order doesn't matter right now, but it will later. Allan, what did you come up with?"

"Integrity. Others first. Intelligence. Belief. Generosity." Allan gauged the room for a reaction.

"What happened to family?" Reggie asked.

"I put it under Others First. I also looked ahead to see where this is going, and I'm already trying to find a peaceful solution to a disagreement we are going to have."

Reggie threw back his head and laughed. "You certainly are intelligent."

"What am I missing?" Matt asked.

"That you're not intelligent," Charlotte deadpanned.

Matt reached his fist across the table towards Charlotte. "Give me a fist bump. I admire your quick gibe."

Charlotte smacked his hand away.

Reggie said, "Before we get to what Allan is talking about, we need to do step four and verbalize. Add a verb to each value so it looks like an actionable core value. Your core values are similar, but I'm guessing your verbs will give a different feel to the value."

Matt started. "Drive expensive cars." He looked at his siblings' reactions. They shook their heads.

"'Drive' is supposed to be a noun," Allan said. "The values are nouns. You used 'drive' as a verb."

"Duh! It was a joke," Matt said. "You didn't get that yet. You're the one with intelligence in your values."

"Ummm, Matt," Charlotte waved her hand in protest of Matt's words. "You should tell people ahead of time when you're about to tell a joke because you're usually serious and don't tell jokes."

"What? I'm funny. Allan?"

"Char's right."

"Ugh. Never mind. Let's start over. Thrust forward with Drive. Flood with Generosity. Fight for Integrity. Infuse Belief."

"Nice recovery," Reggie faux clapped. "Charlotte?"

"Prioritize Respect. I can't think of one for 'drive.' Matt's sounds too driven."

"I wrote 'Focus Your Drive,'" Allan said. "I think we can't all maintain the passion that Matt does. Drive doesn't need to be tempered when it's focused on the right things. But I can't thrust forward all the time with the energy of you two."

"Okay," Charlotte continued, "then I'm going to say Mandate Respect, Direct your Drive. Prioritize Integrity. Inspire Belief. Love through Generosity."

"Before we go to Allan's, let me make a few observations," Reggie said. "I typed out your verbalizations. Look at the TV. I put them side by side. Matt, all of your verbs are forceful, even violent. Thrust, flood, fight, infuse."

"Is that bad?"

"No. It's you. But it's bad if you don't hear Charlotte's verbs."

"I heard them."

Reggie stared at Matt until Matt shifted in his seat.

"Are you implying I didn't?"

"'He who has ears to hear, let him hear.' Ever hear that?"

"In church."

"What does it mean?"

"That some people aren't really hearing the truth that is taught. They need to tune in."

"Correct! Are you hearing Charlotte's verbs?" Reggie picked up the electronic pen and circled each verb as he said it. "Mandate. Direct. Prioritize. Inspire. Love. What do you think about her verbs?"

"That my verbs will get a lot more done. Her verbs aren't as actiony like mine are."

"Does she have any verbs that stick out to you as forceful?"

Matt scanned the list. "Mandate. Sounds a little fascist."

"Matt, what core value is connected to her forceful verb?"

"Respect."

"Why do you think that Respect is the one word that she put with a forceful verb?"

"She really wants it?"

"Why does she really want respect?"

Matt paused. "Ask her."

"You know the answer," Reggie challenged.

"Is it 'because she doesn't think she gets it?'"

Reggie shook his head. "That's not the answer."

"Then I don't know the answer."

Reggie sighed. "The answer is 'because she does not get respect.'"

"Isn't that what I said?"

"No. You said that she thinks she doesn't get it. The answer is that she doesn't get it."

Matt shifted in his chair. Reggie had never been this aggressive.

"So we're talking about Bob?" Matt asked.

Reggie's stare pierced Matt. "First, I'm talking about you."

Matt shot back in his chair. "What?"

Allan stood and held his hands up to the ceiling. "Hallelujah! This needed to be said."

"I don't respect her?" He turned to Charlotte. "I don't respect you?"

Charlotte remained silent, avoiding Matt's gaze.

"Matt, think about what you said. And please, sit down." Reggie sat down next to Matt. "You have great respect for Allan, so your chirping at him earlier surprised me. You don't respect Charlotte. And she values and craves that. If you and Charlotte are going to be leaders here, you must value respect as a company. Yes. Bob is a big respect problem. You're a respect problem, too. I don't think you respect her value. I think you need to push past seeing her as your little sister. I think you suppress her brilliance, and it hurts your company."

Matt looked at Charlotte. Tears dripped off her bowed head.

His throat felt like a rock was stuck in it. He felt small because he had made her feel small. He didn't understand how everyone couldn't want such forceful verbs. But for the first time, it dawned on him how much he devalued what she valued. Her verbs were more tender and more cautious. His stomach sunk with the feeling of having run over his sister.

Matt rose from the chair and knelt by Charlotte's. He embraced her. She leaned into the hug. Her warm tears fell onto Matt's neck and triggered his own tears.

"I'm sorry, Char." He pulled back and looked into her eyes, but he couldn't be sure if she was looking into his eyes because his vision was blurry. "What you feel matters. I'm sorry that it hasn't. I'm really sorry."

Allan knelt by both of them and embraced them in his tremendous wingspan. "I love my family."

Reggie gave them a brief break, though no one left the room. After a few minutes, he said, "Are you ready to get back to it? Allan, we need to hear your verbs."

"I'm ready. Offer Integrity. Lift Others. Act with Intelligence. Persist in Belief. Love through generosity."

"Love it, but I have one question before we move on," Reggie said. "You said 'family' is under others. But you put integrity first. That surprises me. Why did you choose that order?"

"If I'm not whole and true in my life, then what am I offering my family?"

"That's deep!" Reggie sounded impressed. "Next step for everyone is to decide your company's core values. It should be a conglomerate of the owners' core values."

"That's simple!" Matt said. "Drive, Generosity, Integrity, Belief, and…" He looked at Charlotte. "…Respect."

Charlotte beamed.

"Good choices," Allan said.

"Matthew Wellington," Reggie's face grew stern, "are you certain that you are going to run a company where respect is a core value?"

"Yes. I respect my sister. That's why I'm adding it. It's a core value."

"Okay." Reggie raised his eyebrows.

"What's wrong with it?"

"Do you understand what that might mean if someone is disrespectful of others?"

"We will deal with it," Matt nodded with assurance.

"And you're all in agreement?"

The siblings agreed.

"The Core Values of NGC are Drive, Generosity, Integrity, Belief, and Respect," Matt said. "It's cemented."

CHAPTER 19

The Company's Purpose

Reggie flipped the page in his workbook. "Let's turn to page 40. We're going to identify your personal purpose. A fulfilling life gives you daily direction and focuses you toward worthwhile pursuits. So now you're going to brainstorm. Tell me what you love. It's something from your past. Secondly, tell me your gift to the world right now in the present. Third, tell me what you want to be remembered for in the future."

Matt grinned as he wrote the answers. "This is the easiest thing I've done all day."

Reggie wiped his brow. "You needed something easy after the core values."

"Personally," Allan's voice dragged, "I find this as painful. But I'm done."

"Matt, you go first," Reggie said.

"I love helping people solve problems. My gift to the world is my growing knowledge and experience in real estate. I want to be remembered for revitalizing Grant City and leading others to success."

"Great answers! Charlotte?"

"Similar to Matt, I love solving complex problems. I also love organization and structure. My gift to the world? Bringing pieces together and seeing something come to fruition. What do I want to be remembered for? Inspiring people to discover what they are capable of doing."

"Nice! Allan?"

"I love working with numbers and creating family experiences. My gift is bringing organization."

"That's true!" Matt interjected.

"And I want to be remembered for being faithful to and providing for my wife and children. I want to be remembered as a great family man. I want to be remembered for being devout and successful, but not at the expense of my family. I want to be someone who is known as having harmony in life and business.

"Awesome!" Reggie's eyes widened. "Now, everyone will need to simplify a bit, but you need to write a purpose statement by filling in the blanks."

"Simple!" Matt said. "I love solving problems because the world needs REI knowledge because I want to be remembered for revitalizing Grant City."

"Thanks, Matt! Who's next?" Reggie asked.

"I'll go," Charlotte said. "I love solving complex problems because the world needs to see things that can happen because I want to be remembered for inspiring people to discover their capabilities."

"Guess that leaves me," Allan said. "I love numbers and experiences because the world needs organization–including within a family–because I want to be remembered as a man who built a business but not at the expense of his family."

"We're on the right track!" Reggie rubbed his hands together. "Now, we need to do this for the company instead of you as individuals."

"How about as a company? What do you love doing?"

"Restoring," Matt answered.

"Working as a family," Charlotte said.

"What is NGC's gift to the world?"

Allan cleared his throat. "Improving the lives of those in Grant City through rehabbing houses."

"What do you want NGC to be remembered for?"

"Restoring Grant City," Matt answered.

Allan and Charlotte agreed.

"So, what is your company's purpose indicator?" Reggie asked.

"Putting families in homes," Matt said.

Allan added, "But we are trying to build neighborhoods, too."

Reggie offered, "So you put families back into neighborhood homes."

"I'd like to make one improvement on that," Charlotte sat up. "We're a family working to put families back in neighborhood homes."

"Ooooh! I love that!" Matt pumped his fist.

"Char, you are a genius," Allan smiled and nodded in admiration at her.

"That's good, but that's not all. How will you know if you've done it? What's the metric?" Reggie's challenge made Matt stop and think.

"I have a crazy number in my head. I've never shared it," Matt said. "We want to turn 5,000 houses back into homes in the next ten years."

Allan choked on his water. "What?"

Charlotte said, "Wow! That's ambitious. But I'm up to the challenge."

Allan's face soured. "That's 500 per year. That's ten per week. That's two per day."

"Great observation, Allan!" Reggie had that sparkle in his eyes from seeing things come together. "You are seeing the short-term goals that we'll talk about soon."

"Too ambitious?" Matt asked.

"That's a great goal," Reggie applauded. "It should be a stretch goal that drives innovation, narrates the story, and aims for future success."

"Are you two serious?" Allan asked Matt and Charlotte.

"Yes! It's inspiring. This is Inspiration Day," Matt said.

"It is an inspiring goal," Charlotte said.

"You're not inspired, Allan?" Matt asked.

"I'm inspired to get a drink," Allan said.

Charlotte scrunched her face. "You don't drink."

"I know, but this purpose might drive me to it," Allan said.

"We definitely need a break here," Reggie said. "Let's meet back in ten."

CHAPTER 20

The Company's Culture

"This has been an emotional morning," Reggie's compassionate voice comforted Matt. "But it's good and healthy work. You three are doing the right work to surge through this plateau. Now we're going to talk about culture."

"Is this going to be emotional?" Matt asked.

"Might be. You might be lying under your desk in the fetal position by lunchtime!"

"I've never seen Matt broken like that." Allan grinned.

"You'd like that, wouldn't you two?" Matt asked.

"I like unique things," Charlotte offered.

"NGC's culture directly affects growth because uninspired leaders struggle to maintain productivity or achieve growth. We need position affirmation, people affirmation, goal affirmation, and mission affirmation. Affirmation is not 'everyone gets a trophy.' It's not giving in to everyone's desires."

"Then what is it?" Charlotte asked.

"We'll get to that in a bit," Reggie answered. "Right now, please look at page 44. This shows potential versus performance. What's the first thing you think when you look at this chart?"

"I think about where everyone at NGC falls," Matt quickly answered.

"Exactly. And be careful. You can be quick to judge where people fall on here, but remember your own past. Matt, when you worked in Chicago, where did you fall on this chart?"

Matt considered the chart. "I was either high potential or core players. I definitely was not a star or high performer. My performance was middling because I was not given opportunities. No one coached me, and no one invested in me."

"Allan, when you worked at the dealership in college, where did you fall on this chart?" Reggie asked.

"Workhorse. I performed, but I had no potential there. IT wasn't really up my alley. I wasn't inspired."

"Thank you, Allan. So think through this for your current employees. Consider if they are low, middle, or high potential, and consider if they are low, middle, or high performance. They might be like Allan at the dealership. They might be great people who are not great fits in their current positions. Don't denigrate them. Figure out how to affirm them."

"Hey Char!" Matt smirked as he called across the table. "Where would Bob fit on this chart?"

"Bob!" Charlotte bit her lip. "He would be…." Her voice drifted off as she looked at the options.

"Just say it, Char." Matt goaded her. "He would be…."

"He'd be a star," Allan admitted. "Maybe a high performer at worst."

Matt's smirk grew larger as he nodded. "Right, Char?"

She didn't answer. She didn't look at Matt.

"Char," Allan dramatically flipped back and forth between pages, "Matt didn't look at the next page yet."

"What's on the next page?" Matt's smirk disintegrated into concern.

"Great question!" Reggie interjected. "Let's turn there. Page 45. People affirmation. This chart shows trust versus alignment and—"

"See! See it, Matt?" Charlotte dropped her book on the table and poked it with her finger. "Bob is low trust. He's either a bad fit, or low trust, or culture-killing. And each option says, 'Move on!'"

Allan cackled. "That blew up in your face, Matt. On page 44, you're ready to promote Bob, and this page says we should can him."

Matt slumped in his chair. "If you really want low sales and no cash flow to build this up, we can fire him."

"Stop! Stop!" Reggie held up his hands, silencing the conference room. "You are all looking at this wrong."

Allan and Charlotte's smug faces sobered. Matt sighed in relief.

"We're not here to rip on people. But let's talk about Bob. On one chart, he is an asset. On another chart, he is worthy of dismissal. What can you do to work with him to make him an asset for both?"

"I've known him for about fifteen years," Allan said. "He's not going to change."

"Why do you assume he's low trust?" Matt asked.

Charlotte pointed to the book. "It says, 'Culture Killing.' It couldn't be any more perfect of a description."

"But we trust him to make sales," Matt countered.

"We don't trust him with anything else," Allan said.

"The point is to lift up all people," Reggie said. "I'm sure Bob creates real issues, but let's not vilify him. He may be a culture-killing fit, but you need to first see how you can correct that because he has been a big part of your quick turnaround the past three months."

"Truth!" Matt said.

"We don't want to turn this into a gripe session," Reggie warned. "The people outside of this room gripe. The people in this room solve problems. For all employees whom you identify as low trust or low alignment, you have to consider if it's because of your own faults or poor hiring practices. Did you put them in the wrong position? Do you keep them from rising?"

"But what about the other people who suffer under Bob's culture killing?" Charlotte asked.

"Great question. You must consider all of this. There's a Columbia University study that says the likelihood of job turnover at an organization with high company culture is 13.9 percent. What do you think it is at companies with "low" company culture?

"Thirty?" Matt offered.

"Higher."

"Forty?" Allan asked.

"Higher."

"Wow! Fifty?" Charlotte guessed.

"48.9," Reggie answered. "Almost half. This shows the danger of the culture-killer mindset because unhappy employees tend to do the minimum. Employees who *feel* unappreciated quit. That's why they need affirmation. Poor managers create scenarios in which workers are unproductive and unhappy. Conversely, effective affirmation creates positive company culture. *Harvard Business Review* says that a positive culture creates loyal and passionate employees who bring loyal and passionate customers. The happiness keeps spreading."

"When I worked in Chicago," Matt said, "the last straw in my hat was when a customer I had worked with for five years left us. They had been with the company for fifteen years. My boss, Kevin, wouldn't listen to me telling them the client's concerns. It just made the situation untenable."

"Exactly. They had been loyal and passionate customers, but the culture killed it."

"Yes!" Matt smacked the table. "It killed me."

"So, Matt, are you considering if culture is killing people around here?" Reggie asked.

Allan mouthed a "Wow!" without making a sound.

"Before today, I wasn't considering it," Matt confessed. "We definitely have some issues to talk through."

"Thank you for saying that, Matt," Charlotte said.

"Can I give a little more clarity to this?" Reggie asked. "One in 10 workers experience a toxic workplace culture. This means that you might only have pockets of toxic culture. You're not a big business, so one toxic pocket can infect the whole company."

"Reggie, do you think we need to fire Bob?" Matt asked.

"I'm not here to answer that question. You have to develop the culture that makes the answer obvious."

"I like that answer," Allan said. "We don't need Reggie to tell us what to do. We need to agree on what to do."

"Yes!" Reggie said. "You have to learn to implement affirmation correctly and consistently. Then you fine-tune it for NGC."

The siblings looked at each other and nodded.

"Company culture is everything. You'll never completely avoid toxicity and Bobs. But you have to take charge of it. You're not a failure if you have it. You will fail if you don't deal with it."

CHAPTER 21

Systems Day

Matt felt the optimism in the conference room as he walked in for Systems Day. He was ten minutes early, but he was the last one to arrive. Reggie, Allan, and Charlotte were laughing as he walked in. The "Good Morning" greetings felt genuine. Charlotte stood up and hugged him. Some big wrinkles needed to be ironed out, but inside that conference room, the sun seemed to be shining instead of the LED lights.

"Are you ready to get going with systems? Long day yesterday. Hopefully, a little less emotional today."

"Systems have absolutely zero feelings," Reggie joked.

"Good. I'm worn out. On top of that, I kept getting calls last night from Barb about how to do some things."

"Then you need to give her some systems," Reggie said. "You three ready?"

"I'm ready!" Charlotte beamed.

"Let's jump in." Reggie rubbed his hands together. "The Systems quadrant has four elements: effective meetings, stoplight reports, business pipeline, and process execution. This is day-to-day stuff that requires more than visionary chops. It also needs serious mental strength because it must be implemented every day."

"Sounds like it's up your alley, Allan." Matt smiled at Allan, but the smile was not returned. "What's wrong? Not excited?"

"This part of the curriculum can be a little bit of a letdown," Reggie said. "Yesterday had the excitement and exhilaration of setting goals and figuring out how to get the results you want. Today is nitty gritty. Today requires determination to focus."

"Then I might need a second coffee," Matt said.

Charlotte laughed. Matt looked for Allan's reaction. Nothing.

"Speaking of coffee, I went to Starbucks this morning." Reggie held up a cup. "They spelled my name wrong: R-E-J-I. But other than that, they have a good system. That's why they are tops in the coffee market. Systems dominate our lives. We live in a solar system. It structures our days and years. Systems create the space for you to rise. What other systems can you think of?"

"Immune system," Charlotte answered.

"Great one! It keeps us healthy. What else?"

"The Dewey Decimal System," Allan offered.

"What?" Reggie thought a moment. "Oh. The library system."

"You don't use the library anymore, do you?" Allan asked.

Reggie held up his phone. "I do all my reading on here. But that's a great example. Do you know who said this? 'Being busy does not always mean real work. The object of all work is production or accomplishment, and to either of these ends, there must be forethought, system planning intelligence, and honest purpose, as well as perspiration. Seeming to do is not doing.'"

"Thomas Edison," Matt answered.

"History buff?" Reggie asked.

"A little bit."

"I've been to his house and museum in New Jersey. He invented the lightbulb, held over a thousand patents, and–Allan will like this–created the world's first industrial research library."

"A man after my own heart," Allan quipped.

"Did you know that Edison was a man who couldn't manage his own finances and resources? He hired people to do what he was not good at so he could focus on R&D. That's what systems do: they create a community of success, especially when people are in the right seat. Systems are not just important. They are an exciting and crucial component to achieving a RISE trajectory."

"Exciting? I thought that you said today wouldn't be exciting," Charlotte teased.

Reggie shook his finger at her and laughed. "Some people will find that exciting."

"I find this exciting," Allan said, though, as usual, his voice didn't sound excited.

"Thank you, Allan," Reggie said. "Systems can and should be a dynamic, interesting component in your business and your RISE experience. Your ability and enthusiasm for creating effective systems will make or break your momentum."

"I'm confused." Charlotte held up her hand to interrupt. "You said today might be a letdown. But you're using words like 'dynamic' and 'interesting' and 'enthusiasm' to talk about the Systems material."

"Oh good! Someone else gets to experience Charlotte throwing their words back in their face," Matt whispered.

Charlotte threw a waded-up paper towel at him.

"Charlotte, that's a great question," Reggie paused to think. "That's a great question that I am going to explain in future Systems Days."

"Wow!" she gushed. "I will be mentioned at every future Systems Day."

"Today is tough because you have to build the systems. It's tedious. Tomorrows are better because you will eliminate the confusion and shutdowns. You will minimize questions. You will increase direction. People will know what to do each day and for each job. They will like working here."

"Okay. That was a pretty good answer." Charlotte flashed a smile. "I'm excited to work at a place like that!"

"Since I was here in the winter, you started your weekly meetings, right?"

"Yes," Matt said.

"There are four meetings you should hold. If you are going to be an effective RISE leader, I recommend you classify these meetings according to the frameworks I will show you. Employees, managers, and leaders will come to expect a productive experience from a meeting rather than a boring and/or negative one. Any thoughts on what types of meetings there are?"

"Ones where people complain," Matt joked.

"One where we stare at our CEO waiting for direction," Charlotte responded.

Matt laughed. "I've decided to enjoy today. You're not breaking my good mood."

"Shucks!" Charlotte exclaimed.

"Ones where we sit in silence and quiver inside because we're discussing how we will pay our bills?"

"That's so three months ago, Allan," Charlotte said.

Allan added, "I just googled that, and it came up. I wasn't saying it from experience."

Charlotte tried to punch Allan in the arm, but he blocked the blow and rolled her chair away from him with a little kick to the frame.

"I'm going to note that I will no longer ask this question on Systems Day." Reggie feigned writing in his workbook. "The four types of meetings are culture meetings, strategic meetings, organizational meetings, and tactical meetings."

"I was going to say that," Matt said.

"Doubtful," Charlotte replied. "We only have tactical meetings around here, and in those, we discuss if you are going to mud drywall or paint trim that day."

"Now, that is a blast from 'three-months-ago' past. Not doing it anymore," Matt argued.

Reggie continued, "Each meeting has a positive component of growing your business. Each one helps your employees feel like they can RISE. They will feel positive about themselves and their roles in the company and the community."

"So a tactical meeting inspires people because we solve a problem or implement a plan?" Matt asked.

"Exactly!" Reggie paced as he spoke. "The nature of tactical meetings propels us forward immediately. It reminds people what they are doing right now. On the other hand, strategic meetings—like this one today—can be tough. It's good to use personal anecdotes to keep them lively."

"You haven't used too many personal anecdotes," Matt said.

"That's because you three just keep shredding each other. I don't know if you need to be entertained. But I'm entertained by you," Reggie said.

"You're welcome." Matt grinned.

"Anyway," Reggie said, "in strategic meetings, stress the positivity of using them to create future growth through processes, policies, and plans."

"So they're painful, but necessary!" Allan stared back and forth between Matt and Charlotte.

"What are you trying to say, Allan?" Charlotte asked.

Allan put his hands behind his head and reclined. "I like this. We need this. This is my favorite day."

"How do you know? We just started," Matt argued.

Allan shook his head. "Don't care what you say. This is revolutionary for us."

"Yes, it can be revolutionary!" Reggie pumped volume into the conversation. "The average worker spends six hours a week in meetings."

"And we're going to reduce that time?" Charlotte asked.

"No!" Reggie responded. "We're going to make them a productive and inspirational six hours!"

"But how do we make them exciting?" Matt asked.

"Effective meetings are exciting. When your employees understand that the meeting isn't a time suck, then they will be excited because meetings will give focus and solve problems."

"What if the person doing the meeting isn't excited?" Allan asked.

"You need to be positive. Charisma helps, of course. No matter your demeanor, positivity will excite people. You also need to clearly state what the meeting is for, and you need to have each of these meetings at the right interval."

"I'm slightly skeptical that we can make meetings exciting," Allan said.

"I hate to say it, but I think that, too," Matt admitted.

Reggie sang, "I'm going to coach you on how! But first…I need to find the little boys' room."

"Matt's office is two doors down on the left," Charlotte said without skipping a beat.

Reggie and Allan laughed. Matt didn't.

Reggie said, "That scowl on Matt's face tells me we need a ten-minute break. See you in a few."

CHAPTER 22

The Meetings

"Let's get back to it," Reggie sang. "Let's start with culture meetings. What are your culture meetings like around here?"

"Being that we just talked about establishing culture yesterday, they are non-existent," Charlotte said.

"What?" Reggie facetiously feigned shock. "In culture meetings, each person has the chance to contribute their thoughts and opinions."

Charlotte chuckled and scrutinized Matt.

"I fail at that," Matt admitted.

Reggie continued, "You should be hearing from other team members and discovering different perspectives. They build teamwork. These meetings bring cohesion. And you'll often find that you'll find new strategies and improved processes."

"People being heard energizes people," Charlotte said.

"What would that meeting look like?" Allan asked. "It can't be everyone just saying what they want. We might surpass six hours just on that one meeting."

"There's a sample agenda on page 55. Each meeting element is assigned several minutes. First, review core values, the purpose statement, and KPIs. It helps the meeting from becoming a free-for-all and reminds everyone of what your business is about. Then you appreciate your resources, your people. Matt, what's something you appreciate about Allan?"

"Last week, I was concerned about showing appreciation to an investor, and Allan asked if he could take care of it. We got a heartfelt thank-you email from the investor. Allan really thought through how to say thank you, and it was a blessing to NGC."

"Great one!" Reggie said. "Next, share something that inspired you."

"I have one, Reggie." Allan raised a finger. "Matt calling you has inspired me that he wants to find the order that I crave."

"Awww. That's sweet, Allan," Charlotte said. "I would have to agree."

"Then you move on to system successes," Reggie said. "What's an example of that?"

The siblings looked at each other and broke out in laughter. "We don't have one," Matt said.

"Maybe we'll have some after today," Allan said.

"Fair enough," Reggie responded. "Next would be engagement victories where you share a story of a client you helped. I won't ask for any examples since we haven't done Engagement Day yet. Then schedule the next culture meeting."

"I have to say that I see how this can be inspirational and exciting. We don't talk much about successes here. We've all been pinned down with putting out fires most days."

"Exactly!" Reggie continued pacing around the room. "This is energizing. Are you ready to talk strategic meetings?"

"Yes!!!" Allan growled at a volume ten times his normal volume. Charlotte jumped.

"What's going on? This isn't Braveheart," Matt squinted at his brother.

"I was just being funny. Maybe ironic because meetings are supposed to be boring."

"You're really into this, huh?" Matt asked.

"Yes!" Allan pumped his fist.

"Good. Good," Reggie said. "Strategic meetings provide a space for team members to collaborate and brainstorm solutions to current challenges, future goals, and strategies. Focus on strategy and planning to identify key objectives. Discuss ways to best achieve them. Map out a roadmap to success."

"So, we're staying on top of progress and keeping focus on the objectives?" Matt asked.

"It's not just that," Reggie countered. "You create a collaborative environment. You give your team a chance to solve problems and be creative. Let them generate fresh ideas and share valuable insights that you don't see from working here each day."

Allan stood and reached towards the ceiling. "I am energized!"

"So, what do you think are the elements of a strategic meeting?" Reggie asked.

"The greeting?" Matt asked.

"Of course. Greet people and introduce anyone who needs introducing. Then we have core values violations."

"Oooooh. I can't wait to have a strategic meeting!" Charlotte rubbed her hands together.

Matt rolled his eyes.

"Then you have purpose alignment where you identify any products or partnerships over the past quarter that misalign with your stated purpose. Then, KPI review. Then, you audit the four quadrants of RISE. First audit Resources. Ask what personnel challenges you need to address."

"Like when we fire Bob?" Allan grinned at Matt as he stirred a pretend pot on the conference room table.

"Great example," Reggie said.

Charlotte applauded. "So Reggie is saying we should fire Bob!"

"Are you?" Matt asked.

Reggie waved his hands in the air. "You need to figure that out for yourself. Follow the RISE process and decide. Let's move on. You audit Inspiration. Are you inspiring your team through personal interactions and the emotional paycheck?"

"No." All three siblings said it simultaneously.

"But to be fair," Allan added, "it's better than it was before Resource Day."

"You do a Systems audit and ask which systems or processes aren't working and need to be retooled. And then the Engagement audit, where you discuss which marketing channels need adjusting or retooling. Then, schedule your next meeting. Any questions?"

No one answered.

"Then let's move on," Reggie said. "We need to discuss the organizational meeting. This gives your team the opportunity to discuss processes, policies, and plans for the future. Let people have space to offer thoughts and opinions about solutions, problems, and goals. This builds communication. As you grow, you will have team members who don't know how to communicate. They don't know how to collaborate. Some are really poor at making decisions. This gives them a chance to exercise these skills. And for the organization, you are staying on top of trends and changes in your market."

"So we start with a greeting and something positive, right?" Matt laughed.

"Yes. If there's time—and you are daring—you can ask someone else to share."

"Why is that daring?" Allan asked.

"Because some people will just keep talking." Reggie wiped his brow. "Next, you would review The Four: those four important things that must be completed this quarter. Review KPIs. Update the To-Do List from last week's operational meeting. And then you open the floor?"

"Just let people say what they want?" Matt asked. "Sounds daring, as you said earlier."

"Open the floor within RISE," Reggie answered. "Ask them, 'What Resources are missing?' and let them answer. Then ask them if their Inspiration is lacking."

"Okay, but first, we are going to have Inspiration in place. That sounds like a bloodbath in our current climate," Matt said.

"Then ask, 'Are Systems broken?' and listen for the answers. And then ask, 'Is Engagement needed from a customer?' and listen. Then schedule your next meeting."

"So the employees carry the bulk of this meeting?" Charlotte asked.

"Yes!" Reggie gave her a thumbs up. "Then there are tactical meetings. There are two types: daily and weekly. I call the daily a 'Process Huddle.' It's five minutes. Give good news. Give a team update. Review the Key Process Indicators."

"That's it?" Matt asked.

"That's it. In and out, keeping a metric in front of everyone," Reggie answered. "I call the weekly meeting 'Systems 60.'"

"It's an hour long?" Allan asked.

"Correct! Look at page 58. Greet. Give good news. Do an as-is process review. Go over Key Process Indicators and targets. Then, there is process learning, which takes up half the meeting. Then, you document and update the should-be process and create a roll-out plan. Those are your meetings!"

"I'm calling a culture meeting tomorrow morning at 8 a.m.!" Charlotte laughed.

"Not a bad idea. Normally, I would take a break here, but since we took one a little while ago, are you good with pushing through on the Business Pipeline."

Matt's eyes widened. "That sounds like something I would rather get done with sooner than later. Let's push through!"

"Business pipeline. Is this about the time Matt went to fix a leak and broke a pipe on Maple Street?" Allan asked with a straight fist.

Charlotte busted out laughing.

Matt felt flush. "Guys, it was not my fault that the pipe had corroded."

"No, Allan, that is not what I'm talking about," Reggie said. "But that was funny. The business pipeline is where you focus on speeding up the business pipeline as a crucial component of RISE success, using SIPOC, cycle time strategies, and cash conversion cycle analysis."

"We've tried this," Matt said, "but we didn't have the cash to keep it going."

"Yep," Reggie shook his head. "That happens a lot at this point. You are not alone, Matt. Pipeline improvement often breaks down. RISE is different. It's designed to create a support system for other individuals in the company who are RISING along with the business. I thank you for your honesty. I think you are identifying a reason why pipelines stop flowing."

"Because of money?" Charlotte asked.

"Perhaps, but there are more reasons," Reggie answered. "The thing to focus on isn't necessarily money. It's how to speed up your business pipeline. How do you get more deals done? How do you make the time from start to finish shorter?"

No one answered.

"It's not a rhetorical question," Reggie said.

"Have procedures written down," Allan offered.

"Great answer! Who else?"

"Communication improvements?" Charlotte asked.

"Definitely."

"I'm not sure how we'd do it here, but automation is one way," Matt answered.

Reggie nodded. "It sure is. Creating an efficient workflow significantly reduces bottlenecks in your business pipeline and achieves faster turnaround times for projects. Investing in technological tools leads to efficiency, smoother operations, and better results."

"What kind of results?" Allan asked.

"*Harvard Business Review* says that sales pipelines can boost the rate of growth by 15 percent."

"We need more than 15 percent growth!" Matt said.

"Consider this, though," Reggie said. "You aren't optimized in resources and inspiration. How much growth will you have if your Resources are in order? How much growth will you have if your Inspiration is optimized? What if each of those were just fifteen percent increases? With compound gains, that's a 52 percent increase. And we haven't even increased engagement yet. When you increase engagement, you are going to have more business."

"And our pipeline better have a large diameter to allow for flow," Charlotte said.

"Exactly! That's how you should be thinking. More efficient cash conversion cycles will result in higher profits for the company and a better understanding of resource allocation, which leads to overall improved transparency and confidence from top to bottom. You don't want a two-inch drainpipe like you have in your house. You don't want a four-inch sewer pipe. You want a pipe you can walk through."

"Amen!" Matt waved his hand in the air. "There's a lot of flow in that pipe."

"Scary!" Allan said.

"Scary?" Matt asked.

"It's just hard to imagine us doing that compared to how we've operated over the past two years."

"That's fair," Matt said.

Reggie flipped forward a few pages in his book. "We're going to look at some diagrams on pages 61 and 62. They might look complicated right now. Just start at step one and fill them in."

The discussion began, and Matt quickly lapsed into his imagination. He pictured himself in a giant pipe, riding a giant raft through the strong flow of water. Kevin would be hanging onto the side of the raft, begging to get on. Though there were eleven available seats, Matt would tell him that there was no room and then push Kevin off with his oar.

"What are you giggling at? Are you paying attention?" Allan asked.

Matt snapped out of his daydream. "I'm over here doing visionary things. I'm taking a break for a few, but the rest of you can keep going. I'll be right back."

CHAPTER 23

The KPIs

"This day is going well. Don't you think?" Reggie asked as they returned from lunch and into the conference room.

"Not nearly as painful as I thought it might be," Matt said. "You still love it, Allan?"

Allan nodded. "It clarifies a lot."

"It has for me, too," Matt admitted. "It has really helped me think about how to organize people. I have big ideas, but managing people has been challenging."

"Any comments, Charlotte?" Reggie asked.

"I see the value of what we are doing, the value of doing the nitty-gritty now and avoiding problems later."

Reggie nodded. "This can be heavy material. But when you sort it out, it makes everything lighter. Let's move on to Stoplight Reports and KPIs."

"So, is this like where we see red lights and need to stop in our business flow?" Matt asked.

"I'm so glad you asked that! A stoplight actually has three colors: red, yellow, and green. They keep everyone safe on the road as people barrel around in cars that weigh thousands of pounds."

"So the report is telling you when to stop, when to slow, or when to go?" Allan asked.

"Yes. They help you understand and communicate how ideas, concerns, and obstacles can be resolved. You have to leverage the tool in a way that provides clear metrics and feedback that helps everyone RISE. You use them to create growth and growth opportunities based on predetermined metrics and standards."

"How do we determine the metrics?" Charlotte asked.

"You ask great questions. All three of you do. The answer is that you determine the metrics by your KPIs."

"Have we talked about those already?" Matt asked.

"I mentioned them as part of your meetings. And yesterday, Matt, you told us your Key Purpose Indicator. That's where you start."

"I did? I don't remember."

"You said, 'We want to turn 5,000 houses back into homes in the next ten years.' I wrote it down. And then Allan choked on his water and broke that down to two houses per workday. Charlotte then said that she was up for the challenge."

"Did I say that out loud?" Matt asked coyly, touching his chest and feigning surprise.

"You did!" Reggie said.

"You did," Allan lamented.

"That's your Key Purpose Indicator: Turning 5,000 houses back into homes in the next ten years."

"You said there are KPIs, as in, a multiple of them," Matt said. "So we need more than one Key Purpose Indicator?"

"No!" Reggie's deep voice bellowed. "The P changes. The next KPI is the Key Profit Indicator."

"Wait! Wait!" Allan waved his hands in the air. "I can't move forward yet. Are we locked into the purpose being 5,000 houses in ten years."

"No, you're not. You should review the Key Purpose Indicator every three months. It's okay to change them."

Allan exhaled slowly. "Thank you. That will give me a chance to talk some sense into the two of them. So the Key Profit Indicator is how much revenue goal we set over a time period?"

"Exactly!" Reggie turned to Matt and Charlotte. "He's very valuable."

"Thank you!" Allan smiled.

"The next KPI is the Key Performance Indicator. How do you know if you have performed?"

"If we rent or flip a house?" Charlotte timidly answered.

"Yes! So, performance is based on how many houses become occupied through sales or rent. You decide what has to be done on a weekly basis to hit 5,000 houses in ten years."

"Key Performance Indicators are weekly?" Charlotte asked.

"Yes! Key Purpose Indicators are reviewed Quarterly. The Key Profit Indicator is reviewed Monthly. There's a chart on page 66. You keep track and review and adjust every quarter. The Key Performance Indicator is reviewed weekly. Look at the chart on page 67. You keep track weekly, and then monthly, you review and adjust."

"What's the last one?" Matt asked.

"The Key Process Indicator."

"We measure it daily? And adjust it at the weekly meeting?" Matt asked. "I noticed the pattern."

Reggie beamed. "You are a star student."

"But what are we measuring here?" Allan asked.

"It's different for every business. It might be 'How many appointments did we go on this week?' or 'How many leads did we follow up on?'"

"I see how this comes together," Allan leaned back and looked at the screen. "So in the daily meeting—the tactical meeting—we discuss the previous day's process numbers, right?"

"Yes!" Reggie said.

Allan nodded. "So we need to decide the processes that we are going to measure?"

"Yes. That is next. And you must map those processes. This leads us into our next quadrant: Process Execution. The first step under that is Process Mapping."

"Before we move on, could we go back to the Key Process Indicator?" Charlotte asked.

Matt could read the ferocity in her eyes. He worried about what she was about to say.

"Of course," Reggie answered.

"We are going to decide what processes we will chart. So everyone has to have daily process numbers?"

"They do!"

"And they have to report these numbers daily?"

"Or you need a way of collecting the data. It depends on the company and business type and software capabilities."

"What are you getting at?" Matt asked impatiently.

"I don't think Bob is going to report daily numbers," she beamed. "I'm not sure if he'll make it in this new system."

Allan slapped the table and laughed. "This sounds like how they nailed Al Capone on tax evasion instead of murder. You are ruthless, Char. I'm glad you are on my side."

"Wait. Just wait." Matt waved his hands in the air. "You're trying to figure out a way to rig Reggie's RISE system to make Bob quit?"

"No," Allan said. "She's pointing out that this system has a good chance of giving good reason to fire him."

Charlotte pointed at Allan. "Yessssss!"

Matt shook his head. "Wow! No words."

"Let's start Process Execution before we have a civil war," Reggie laughed.

"From Bob's execution to Process Execution. Nice segue, Reggie," Allan joked.

Charlotte snorted. Reggie grinned. Matt glared at his brother and sister.

"If you look at page 71…" Reggie paused and laughed again. "That was just wrong, Allan. On page 71, you see the Nine Box for processes. On the vertical axis, you see the word *Valuable*. That is asking what is valuable externally to the customer. On the horizontal axis, you see the word *Essential*. This is asking what is essential internally to the business. Here's the question. What is a valuable and essential process that you can map and track daily?"

"Going on appointments to view properties," Charlotte offered.

"Brilliant, Charlotte! The more you go on, the more likely you are to buy a property. Of course, you don't want to go to any and all appointments. You need to discern if you will go before you go. We will build that into the process. But your people in acquisitions—like Bob—need to go on appointments. Start tracking how many they do. Review it every day."

"We can do that. That makes so much sense," Charlotte said.

"Page 72 has a procedure guide. We are going to break down appointments into steps. On page 73, we have policy timelines. Processes are what we do. Procedures are how we do it. Policies are a service-level agreement that tells us when we do it. If you look at page 74, it shows you an example of productivity studies. This specific one is about getting leads. That's a vital process, too. It shows you how to examine who might need more training or if feedback is needed."

"So, let's take five, come back, and do the nitty-gritty of laying out these procedures," Reggie said. "I'll mostly work with Charlotte on this since she's the COO. And then we'll wrap it up for today."

Matt skipped laying out the procedures since Reggie said he would mostly work with Charlotte. He sat in his office, a little dead to the world. The information was a lot to take in. He considered his leadership or lack of it. He had a great vision. He was an okay storyteller. He was not a great communicator unless everything was going well.

He opened the vertical blinds in his office. From his office, he could see into the conference room. Charlotte and Reggie were going back and forth, discussing, typing, and pointing at the procedure that Reggie was building on the screen as Charlotte directed. Her face was taut as she thought. It conveyed intelligence.

More intriguing to Matt was Reggie's reaction to her. Reggie was a genius coach and mentor, and he looked engaged with Charlotte like he was talking to a peer. From afar, it looked like there was a respectable exchange of ideas.

Allan stuck his head into Matt's office. "You know that you're the owner and don't need to spy. You could just go in there."

Matt cracked a smile. "But I would interrupt Charlotte."

Allan shrugged. "You've cut her off at least a dozen times in the past two days. Why start being polite now?"

"Maybe I'm a little short at times. What I mean is that I'm watching her and Reggie connect. He looks like…." Matt's words trailed off.

"Reggie looks like he thinks that Charlotte knows what she is doing?"

"Yes! I think that's what it is."

"Like maybe she has good ideas?"

"That is what's going on, isn't it?"

Allan shook his head. "You're blinder than I thought. I'm going in there. Looks like they are wrapping it up."

Matt grabbed his cup and followed Allan into the conference room.

Reggie looked at his watch. "Ready to wrap this up?"

"Ready to hit it running tomorrow," Matt said.

"With a culture meeting where you explain what happened these last two days?" Reggie asked.

"Yes. How did procedures go?"

Reggie gestured to Charlotte. "How did it go?"

"Fantastic. I think we have some procedures in place, and we can start implementing them. Reggie has given me a lot of direction for documenting more procedures and reducing timesucks around here."

"She's a natural," Reggie said. "Operations are in good hands."

Matt sat in his usual spot.

Reggie sat at the head of the table. "Here's how we wrap this up. Hold a culture meeting tomorrow. Announce that you are going to start measuring Key Process Indicators and tell your employees to have the numbers ready on Monday and every day thereafter."

"Charlotte, do you want to talk about that at the meeting?" Matt asked.

"Oh!" She thought for a moment. "I assumed you would do it."

"I did, too. Until I thought about how you are the supervisor of those who are giving you the numbers."

"Sure." She looked confused. "Thanks."

"That's a great idea, Matt," Reggie said. "Take some things off you. That's a perfect metric for Charlotte to oversee. You need to start running the four types of meetings. Do you remember what they are?"

"Quarterly culture meeting with the Key Purpose Indicator. Give everyone a chance to talk," Matt said.

"Quarterly strategic meetings with Key Profit Indicators. That's my meeting!" Allan answered.

"Weekly organizational meeting with Key Performance Indicators," Matt said.

"And the daily tactical meetings with Key Process Indicators," Charlotte said.

"Perfect." Reggie applauded.

"When do you come back for Engagement Day?" Charlotte asked.

"I next come for a quarterly meeting in the late summer. Then sometime after that, I come for Engagement Day."

Charlotte choked up. "Your being here has been great for us. Thank you."

"You still have to do the work," Reggie laughed. "You have some hard days ahead of you. It's only just begun."

CHAPTER 24

The Culture Meeting

"You ready for the culture meeting?" Allan popped his head into Matt's office.

Matt exhaled to slow his breathing. "Our first culture meeting. Casting the new vision. I'm excited. And scared."

Allan raised his eyebrows and closed the door. "My big brother is scared? What's up?"

"We're embarking on a new way to organize NGC. I need the employees to believe in it. I can't explain it all like Reggie could. Last night, as Jean and I were laying in bed, I practiced my explanation on her."

"Did she get it?" Allan asked.

"Two-thirds of the way through it, she started snoring."

"It was probably a long day with the kids. Every day can get kind of long for a stay-at-home mom."

"No doubt, but it didn't help my ego." Matt smiled.

"Do you need me to say anything?"

"No."

Allan wiped his forehead. "Good."

Matt chuckled at his brother. "Do you think it's dumb that I'm worried about Charlotte explaining her part?"

"What are you worried about? She's eager to do it."

"I've never had to trust Charlotte like I now need to trust her in NGC. And speaking of Charlotte, the Bob situation is extra stress."

"Are you laying out clear expectations today?" Allan asked.

"Yes."

"Maybe he will abide by them."

"I hope so. His numbers are so good."

"Right now, the important number is zero," Allan grinned.

"What number is zero?"

"The number of nerves Charlotte has remaining for Bob."

"That certainly settles *my* nerves!" Matt stood up and picked up his laptop.

"Before you go," Allan said, "I want to tell you something. Last night, Lisa and I were talking about RISE and the last two days, and I told her that I've never seen you more realistic, sober, and humble about what we are doing. There have been days when I wondered if we would make it. I wondered if you would lose it. But here you are with a coach and a plan. Congratulations."

"If I could contact feelings other than my nervousness right now, I might have gotten teary-eyed. Allan, I couldn't do this without you."

Allan twisted his shoulders and shriveled up a little.

"You okay with what we are doing, Allan?" Matt asked.

Allan pointed to his watch. "Time to start the meeting. I can answer that later."

Matt and Allan walked into the conference room. Charlotte and the other employees sat around the table. The online call with three virtual assistants was on one screen at the front of the room. Bob was seated next to where Matt usually sat. Matt continued to the front of the room as

Allan sat down next to Charlotte in the spots where they had been during RISE coaching.

Matt was about to begin, but it struck him that someone at the table didn't belong. A mop of blondish hair squeezed from a camo Mossy Oak hat. "What is Plumber Stan doing here?"

Plumber Stan blushed.

Charlotte squeezed his hand. "I wanted him here for this."

Seated on Stan's other side, Barb said, "Stanley is practically family. He's done so many jobs for us."

"Plumber Stan, you have been a good friend to us." Matt breathed deeply and started. "It was almost four months ago when things at NGC hit rock bottom for me. I was overwhelmed. If you know me, you know how hard it is to be vulnerable and say that. I didn't know what to do. And people like you," Matt motioned around the table, "were depending on New Grant City to pay you."

"We haven't missed a paycheck," Barb offered.

"Thanks for saying that. But I want you to have more than a monetary paycheck here. I want you to have an emotional paycheck. There's an emotional component for me. You might know the story, though I don't like talking about it. But today's a new day, so I will.

"Allan, Char, and I grew up around here like all of you. Well," Matt turned towards the camera to talk to the virtual assistants, "except for John, Mylen, and Cyndi. You grew up in the Philippines."

Everyone laughed.

"Be happy you didn't grow up with Midwest winters!" Allan shouted towards the camera.

"Things really started to change around here in my senior year of high school. Allan and I were big into basketball. I always dreamed of being Mr. Basketball, but I was never that good. James Burks was, though. He was a Mr. Basketball finalist and had a Division I scholarship offer. That summer after we graduated and before we had the chance to be college freshmen, he was shot and killed. Right next to me. We were outside the movie theater on Broadway and Fisher. It was the first gang shooting in Grant City. But James and I weren't part of any gang. He was just caught in the crossfire. There have been many days I think about how it could have been me. There have been dark days when I wish it was me."

Matt lowered his eyes to avoid making eye contact with his siblings. He felt like he had said more than he would ever want to say to another human being. But there was a landslide inside of him that felt like freedom in a way he had never experienced in his career.

"Drugs were on the rise in Grant City. Over three years later, while driving home from volunteering at their church's substance abuse program, my parents were killed by a driver high on meth. Charlotte, you were in junior high. I was away at college. Allan had already married and was going to college locally. And he basically became your dad. Not that he was trying to replace Dad. No one could.

"There has been a part of me that has wanted to be a savior to come in and redeem Grant City. Neighborhoods continue to fail. It sometimes looks and feels like there's an eclipse over Grant City that blocks out the refreshment and nourishment of the sun.

"I graduated college and went to work in Chicago. I met Jean, and we got married. But I always had this mission, this goal, in the back of my mind. Some of you know Mrs. Burks, James' grandmother. She is one of our tenants. I want our tenants to have decent neighborhoods. Her daughter, Gloria, is a junkie. I want her to find healing. I want the death of James and Mom and Dad to not be just a tragedy, an afterthought, or meaningless. I wanted it to give me energy, purpose, and drive.

"So I talked to Jean and asked her about leaving Chicago, where she grew up, and coming to Grant City, which is somewhere between

Indianapolis and a cornfield. If I ever doubted that she loved me, I had none after she agreed to go all in on this crazy venture.

"And Allan came along. And he insisted that Charlotte come along. And today, I'm glad he insisted and that she came. I couldn't have done this without either of them.

"When I felt like NGC hit rock bottom, it was painful because I had failed Allan. I had failed Charlotte. I had failed our contractors. I even failed to pay Plumber Stan. I failed James. I failed Mom. I failed Dad. And in a fit of rage, I was providentially reminded of a business coach I had idolized. And I reached out to find out the impossible: if he had an opening. And, again, it had to be the hand of God; someone had canceled on him fifteen minutes earlier when my inquiry came across his computer.

"And Reggie Singer came out and taught us about Resources. And I realized that I tried to do too much. I had little faith in you. I was controlling. He told us to start weekly meetings where we looked at the numbers until he came back. Reggie was here the last two days and talked about Inspiration and Systems.

"We determined Core Values for our business. From now on, our business revolves around these core values: Drive, Generosity, Integrity, Belief, and Respect. We will be driven. We will be generous in our business. We will do all of our work with integrity. We will champion belief. We will respect each other. I don't say this as a threat, but if you don't value those things, we will end up going our separate ways. You eventually won't want to be here."

Matt scanned the employees to see if he had lost any. Their heads nodded. Their faces smiled. They were connected to his words. Even Bob.

"We have a purpose. We are a family working to put families back in neighborhood homes."

Several people clapped. Someone said, "I like it."

"The next question is, 'How will we know if we have accomplished that?' The answer is that we want to turn 5,000 houses back into homes in the next ten years. That's our Key Purpose Indicator."

Allan winced like he did the other times he heard it. The other employees looked back and forth at each other with confusion.

"That's a great goal, Matt!" Bob said. "That's two houses per weekday for the next ten years. Yes! We can do that."

Charlotte winced. "Actually, I agree with Bob. It's ambitious but doable."

Barb raised her hand. "We are going to do that. That's like almost five times what we do right now."

"We're going to grow in personnel, Barb. Bob has already been increasing our sales."

That answer didn't seem to satisfy anyone as discontent grew across several faces.

"Can I speak honestly?" Barb said.

"Of course," Matt answered. "In a culture meeting, you are always free to speak."

"There's too much confusion here most of the time. It's going to be hard to grow," Barb said.

"I don't disagree. On the second day, the Systems Day, we talked through meetings and metrics and establishing procedures. I'll let Charlotte talk about that. But before I turn this over to her, I have an announcement to make."

Allan and Charlotte looked at each other with confusion.

"I haven't talked to Allan and Charlotte about this, but I have a goal for us. It isn't one of the goals that Reggie helped us set. The movie theater on Fisher and Broadway. I want to investigate its ownership with the city and buy it sometime between a year or two from now. I want NGC to turn it into the James Burks Community Center. I want redemption. I want to make the community center the nucleus of revitalizing that neighborhood. In future meetings, we are going to talk about working that into our numbers. This means everything to me about the mission of being a family working to put families back in neighborhood homes."

Matt felt himself choke up. He felt naked and vulnerable in front of the people he led. Exposed, he had shared his heart.

No one said anything.

"Can I say something?" Bob asked.

"Yes," Matt said.

"That's beautiful, Matt. You are trying to put the 'neighborhood' in by putting families back in neighborhood homes. Let's clap for Matt." Bob started applauding, and the rest soon followed.

"Thanks, Bob. Charlotte? You ready."

Matt stepped away from the front of the room and motioned for Charlotte to fill the space. She ascended to the front, dressed a little more like a businesswoman than an artist. She wore a blazer. Matt didn't think she had ever worn one to work. She had straightened her hair and sharply parted it from her left side.

"I feel a little too shocked by Matt's dream to just jump right into the nuts and bolts. Wow, Matt! I love it. You talk about how you are emotionally repressed." Charlotte smiled at Matt. "Lesson number one: You can't just drop an emotional bomb on people and expect them to be business as usual."

Matt bowed. "My apologies. Lesson learned."

"Well, back to business as usual. We plan to implement four types of meetings. The culture meeting is quarterly, where we evaluate and adjust our key purpose indicator, which is turning 5,000 houses back into neighborhood homes in the next ten years.

"We then have a monthly strategic meeting where we consider our Key Profit Indicator. We will look at the financials for the month and see if we are headed towards our goal.

"Next, we have a weekly organizational meeting where we look at our Key Performance Indicator. We consider if we've put any families into homes since that is our goal. This is essentially how many houses or units did we buy and sell or rent this week.

"Lastly, we will start having a daily Tactical Meeting where we look at our Key Process Indicators. Yesterday, I spent two hours with Reggie, hammering out some of our procedures for acquisitions. In order to buy, sell, and rent houses, we have to make calls, send emails, send texts, and go on appointments to see the houses. On Monday, we will hold our first daily tactical meeting at 9:15 a.m. We will meet every day at this time. You need to bring the number of calls and emails and texts and appointments you have made to the meeting."

Bob turned away from Charlotte and to Matt. "So, this is like Charlotte looking over our shoulder now?" Bob asked.

"I'll let Charlotte answer." Matt motioned to his sister.

"No," Charlotte stumbled over several words. The happiness drained from her face. She looked in Bob's direction. "We think these are the key processes in buying and selling, so we want to chart them and see if there is a cause and effect. And if there isn't, we want to figure out what process is driving the acquisitions and sales. When we find it, we want to amplify it so we can turn 5,000 houses back into homes in the next ten years."

Bob huffed. "Matt, the numbers have been great since I've been here. I feel like she is messing with the magic that we've been developing at NGC." Bob pointed back and forth between himself and Matt.

"We're not looking over shoulders, but we don't want private secret sauce. We want to know what you are doing to be successful and sharpen our process and your process. So that way, we'll all be successful together."

Bob nodded. "And she's in charge of the numbers."

"Yes. She is your boss. We love your drive, Bob. That's one of our core values." Matt slowly met the eyes of each employee in the room. "And we need everyone here to work with the core value of respect. That is respect for the new systems and respect for each other."

Matt locked eyes with Bob. Bob squinted and said, "Understood." His neck turned a hot red, and his eyes burned with anger. "May we talk about his afterward?"

"Of course. But for now...." Matt moved to the front of the room and put his arm around Charlotte. "Think about how you can gather those numbers as you go through the next two days and bring them to the 9:15 on Monday morning. You are dismissed."

The room cleared out. Bob lingered.

"Matt, this is a little much. You and me have just started getting NGC out of the gutter."

"Is no one else helping?" Matt asked.

Bob waved away Matt's question. "Sure. Sure. But can you imagine the next few months as I learn more? This tactical meeting and gathering numbers are just going to take away from me making a deal or two each week. I understand what you are trying to do, but we've developed our own system on our raw talent. You and me...we are superstars. We can build this bigger than Reggie and RISE and Charlotte using our gut instincts."

"This feels like in Return of the Jedi when Darth Vader tells Luke that they can rule the galaxy as father and son. The assumption there is that they can depose the Emperor."

Bob's eyebrows raised, exaggerating the lines in his forehead. "Perhaps. Yes. Like that."

"So what happens to Charlotte in this scenario?"

"Oh. She oversees things like she is now."

"Just not you?"

Bob twisted his neck. "You love basketball, right?"

"Yes!"

"You ever see two guys who are bulldog warriors that have been sweating and shoving each other and battling under the boards for the first three quarters? They dive for the same ball that is going out of bounds, or one fouls the other, so they start shoving."

Matt slowly nodded, wondering where this was going. "I have."

"You know how they have lady refs in the NBA now? Those lady refs aren't breaking up two ballers who are about to go at it."

"And your point is?"

"You know."

"That Charlotte is a lady ref Emperor Palpatine that we need to depose so we can rule NGC like father and son ballers?"

Bob chuckled. "You're mixing metaphors."

Matt slowly exhaled. He pulled out his wallet. "Here's $500. Why don't you finish up what you need to for the week—including tracking your numbers—and get away for a night and do something fun and think about what you really want to do and if you really mean what you are saying. Even if you don't come in tomorrow, that's fine."

Bob stepped back. "Are you suspending me?"

"No. I really like you. You are valuable. You were kind to me when we were at the dealership. I want you to be part of what we are doing. And we declared today what we are doing. I want you to clear your head and decide if you are part of it." Matt held out the money.

Bob took it. "Okay. I could stand a day or two away."

"There was a lot to take in from this meeting. I respect you. I want to be generous towards you. Our core values. Let me know if you need me to cover anything for you. And have your numbers ready for Monday at 9:15."

CHAPTER 25

The Tactical Meeting

Matt texted Charlotte at 8 a.m. on Monday morning. *"Not coming in until after the tactical meeting. I want you to run it and not have my presence hanging over it. You are in charge!"*

Matt had slept in a little later that morning. The kids were still asleep, and Jean had gone to the gym. He planned to show up at 9:30. The tactical meeting should only be ten minutes. He figured it would be a little longer on its first day.

The moment he wrote the text, he second-guessed himself. Releasing control always unnerved him. Perhaps he should show up. He was counting on Bob to be a good soldier today.

Jean opened the front door, gave him a kiss, and hopped in the shower. Matt gathered his laptop, phone, and keys. He dressed and stood by the door, waiting for Jean to be done in the bathroom and available to care for the kids should they wake up.

Jean exited the bathroom in a robe and a towel wrapped around her head. She scrutinized her husband. "I thought you were going in later to give Charlotte a chance to run the new meeting. If you leave now, you'll be at work before 8:45."

Matt fidgeted. He twirled his keys around his finger. "I just…ummm…I want to…." He shook his head, unsure what to say.

"I think you should go. You're wound up. But don't go to work. Drive around. Calm down. Maybe go walk in a park."

"It's too hot outside. I don't want to go to work sweaty."

"Matt, can I tell you something? Something serious?" Jean adjusted the collar on his photo.

"Is it going to be emotional or sentimental? Or correcting?"

"Yes."

He nodded at her.

"I met you when you were almost 23. You were on fire for your firm. You were absorbed by it. We dated for four years before you even proposed. My family and friends would ask me why I stuck with you because you didn't seem to have the time to give me like a boyfriend should."

"I've heard this before."

"It's leading somewhere. You went through some dark times at the firm. But you stashed away money so you could give me a good life. People who didn't hang around you much didn't see the man who wanted to lift people up. They saw the driver, the steam roller. I don't think I've ever said this part. Do you know why I think you fell in love with real estate?"

"To be my own boss?"

"I don't think that's why."

"To get out from under Kevin?"

"I don't think that's the real answer either."

"Then why?"

"Juan Perez. Because the day you met Juan Perez, you saw a free man. You saw a man who bought twenty-dollar take-out meals and handed them to homeless people. You saw a man who had the freedom to be generous. I remember the days of you standing up for people to Kevin.

You were so good at your job that you earned that capital to defend them to him. When you are good, you are a helper, and you want to lift people up. In Juan, you saw the chance to be the free man you wanted to be."

"Am I? Do you think I am that free person?"

She looked him squarely in the eye. "No."

"Why not?"

"Because you are standing by the door, swinging your keys, second-guessing your decision to let Charlotte have some power and freedom. You want to take it back. Free people don't steal freedom from others. There's a line between being a controlling dictator and a leader. And I think it's the freedom of that person."

"Are you saying that I'm becoming like Kevin?"

"No. But you have the potential to. I don't want you, too. I love you."

"I love you, too."

"I believe that," Jean said. "Do you know why?"

"Why?"

"Because for the past three or four months, you have worked to improve the business. I don't want you being the guy who is gone all hours. I know there are times it will happen, but lack of success is hard on you. It's unhealthy for you. And I think you realized that. I think you saw how little we were connecting at times. How the kids need you. I think that deep down, you knew you were making Allan and Charlotte miserable."

"All true. I think we're doing better. I'm doing better with the kids."

"You are."

"Thank you. I think Allan feels chained. I sense it. I think Charlotte feels it, too."

"You're like a helicopter parent around her."

Matt nodded. "I am."

"But do you know what else you are? You are the man who wants to redeem the movie theater. I love that about you. You are the man who is trying to succeed for yourself and me and the kids. You are the man who is trying to help his family reach success. I love that about you. They want success, but maybe they don't want to be dragged to it. Everyone doesn't work at your speed or intensity."

"Makes sense. I can see that."

"You are the man who gave $500 to Bob. Not as a negotiating or strong-arm tactic, but because you truly want to make things work with him and because you care about him as a human being. That's who you are."

"He's really helped us with the start of this turnaround. I hope it works out."

"If it doesn't, the next days will be tough." She stroked his face. "But you are on the right path. It might not come when you want. You might have to wait an extra 45 minutes to go to work sometimes."

Matt laughed. "You've just taken up ten of them."

She playfully shoved him. "I love you, Matt. Now go. Drive around. Get a drink. Listen to music. Think. Whatever."

"I love you, too. I will go before you shove me again, and the neighbors think you're kicking me out."

Matt left and meandered towards the interstate. He drove on it until no signs of a city or suburb remained. There were just farms and windmills, cows, and silos. Matt got off the next exit and headed back to Grant City.

At 9:23, Matt's phone alerted him to Charlotte's text.

"Bob didn't show."

Matt was ten minutes away.

"Be there soon."

The phone rang. It was Allan.

"Hello?"

"Matt, you know the assistant I have, Aaliyah?"

Matt laughed. "Yes. She's worked for us for a few months. There are less than a dozen people in the office. I actually know all of them."

"She discovered something troubling. I'll put her on speakerphone."

"Hi, Matt!" Aaliyah's voice bubbled as usual. It certainly didn't sound like something was troubling. "Last week, Charlotte was talking about the Key Process Indicators for acquisitions. Though I am interning in finance, I started thinking about how my department might gather some metrics for acquisitions other than the emails and calls, etcetera."

"I like your initiative!"

She giggled. "Thank you! This whole opportunity is so exciting for me. And I like Allan. He's like my dad."

"So, what is troubling my brother?"

"I was thinking through what financial metrics are connected to our processes. I started looking through expenditures and, specifically, credit card statements. On Bob's credit card this cycle, he has 53 charges for title work at $250 per charge."

"What?!" Matt stepped hard on the gas. "He's only bought 8 houses."

"Actually, it's nine. So I asked Allan if nine purchases out of 32 charges for title work was any kind of process indicator."

"I choked on my bagel!" Allan shouted in the background.

"Thirty-two? I thought you said he had 53 charges."

"I did. He charged 21 of them on Friday."

Matt released the death grip he had on his steering wheel. "Friday? What is he trying to do? That's over thirteen thousand dollars."

"To be exact, it's $13,250. Allan said that we shouldn't do title work until we have an agreement in place."

"Well, Allan is exactly right."

"Hey!" Allan yelled in the background. "Bob is walking in right now."

"I'll be there in a few minutes." Matt ended the call and zoomed towards the office.

He rushed through the front door to find Charlotte and Bob arguing as everyone else stood in the common area and watched. Bob's back was to Matt. Charlotte's face was angry with tears.

Bob repeatedly pointed his finger at her as he said, "And just because you dress a little nicer and put on some makeup and trot your boyfriend around here doesn't mean you know what you are doing in real estate and sales. I'm not giving you process numbers. I know what's going on here. You talked Matt into this so that you can figure out what makes me so successful and copy that and get rid of me!"

Everyone looked to Matt. Bob slowly turned around as it dawned on him that Matt was behind him.

Matt felt himself go into beast mode. He released his clenched fists and took a beat to breathe. "Why did you charge title work 21 times on Friday?"

"Because I am going to personally get you to two houses per day very soon. I'll get you your Key Purpose Indicator. I can do it. You don't need RISE and Charlotte's little numbers and Reggie's plan. Do you know what I did on Friday when you told me to take the day off? I closed three deals. Three!"

Bob slapped three folders on the table in front of Matt.

Matt leafed through the folders.

"That's five for the week. That's halfway to your goal. Who else in acquisitions has done that? Matt, we can do this. I wanted to show you that you and I can do this. I've worked here less than three months, and last week, I personally—me!—acquired five of the ten houses to meet your purpose goal. And we're going to piddle with these process goals that give your little sister a taste of power and importance?"

In his peripheral vision, Matt could see Allan putting his arm around Charlotte. Matt refused to look at Charlotte. He didn't want to see her grief and flip out. "What does that have to do with 21 charges for title work? Did you reach an agreement on 21 houses?"

"No."

"So this is for houses you've looked at and made an offer on?"

"No."

"What? You are doing title work on houses you are interested in? You've spent over ten thousand dollars this month on houses for which we never had an agreement?"

"Yes! There are strategic advantages to doing it. And if I can get at least one extra house out of it, you are getting a lot more back than ten thousand dollars with that one house! You want an appointments metric, but I'm only going on the appointment if there are no title work issues. I'm not wasting my time otherwise."

Matt finally looked at Charlotte. She bit her lip. Her face was taut with anger. Allan met his gaze and nodded as if to say, "You know what has to happen."

The faces of the other employees were a mix of confusion, frustration, and anger.

"Aaliyah?"

"Yes. Write a check to Bob for these three houses he negotiated. Add twenty percent. Give him the check when he hands you his credit card and key because...." Matt turned to Bob. "You are fired."

"That's foolish! You're throwing away greatness." Bob screeched.

Matt ignored Bob and spoke to his staff. "I want you to realize that we are committed to drive. Bob has it. We are also committed to integrity and respect. Bob has neither and has continually proven he has no respect for my little sister." Matt made air quotes. "Those are our core values."

"So I'm the sacrificial lamb for your new fascist organization!"

Matt held out his hand. "Card and keys."

Bob opened his wallet and pulled out the card. He threw it and his keys on the table. Aaliyah handed Bob the check. Bob stormed towards the door. Before he made it to the door, the staff began to applaud and cheer. Bob turned and said something that probably wasn't nice, but Matt couldn't hear it over the cheering. Bob shooed the entire staff and exited.

Allan howled. "Let's carry Matt on our shoulders to the breakroom and celebrate with donuts!"

Matt swatted at his brother. "No one's picking me up."

Charlotte hugged him and buried her head in his chest. "Thank you. I love you."

"I love you, too, Charlotte. I believe in you. Belief. That's our core value."

"We need to hire someone to replace Bob," Allan said.

Charlotte twirled her finger in her hair. "I may already have been looking into that and might have some leads."

Matt laughed. "You do need to be in the HR seat right now."

Allan started clapping to get everyone's attention. "Alright! Everyone get back to work. I don't drink, but I might buy everyone drinks at lunch. Maybe we should take a half day and celebrate like it's D-Day."

"Ding-dong, the Bob is dead!" Barb pumped her fists in triumph.

Matt looked down at his sister. "I think I underestimated the hatred for Bob."

"At least you've seen it now. You heard Allan—back to work." Charlotte headed for her office.

Matt wandered to the front glass doors. In the parking lot, Bob walked back and forth, gesturing with his free hand as he talked on his cell phone.

"You worried about him?" Allan stood next to Matt, staring out the window.

"You mean like he'll get violent?"

"Yes."

"No."

"That he'll seek revenge?"

"I could see that. But doesn't 'revenge' imply that we've done something wrong that needs to be repaid?"

"That's deep."

For a few moments, they stood in silence.

Allan broke the silence. "You did the right thing."

"I did. But it took me too long. I wanted him to work. I wanted to have the procedures in place and let him follow them or not follow them. And if he didn't follow them, he fired himself."

"He did today. He purposefully violated our core values repeatedly. You did the right thing."

"Thanks, Allan."

Allan put his arm around Matt. "I have great peace right now. I have peace that you are going to make this happen."

"We. We will make this happen."

Allan grunted. "But that is half our goal walking out the door. Five houses last week!"

"I know. I wanted to say it. I'm glad you did. I didn't want to sound insensitive. It's nice to be the hero, but we still have to acquire and renovate and flip or rent and pay everyone."

CHAPTER 26

The Procedures

"Wow! It's already 8:00," Matt yawned and laid his head on the conference room table. "Is it too late for coffee?"

"Another twelve-hour day!" Charlotte laughed.

"Are you being serious or facetious? I can't tell."

"Well, we've done a lot of them lately, but we are coming to the end. Getting the policies and procedures in place has energized people like Barb."

Matt sighed. "You didn't answer my question. Serious or facetious?"

Charlotte pursed her lips and looked for the answer on the ceiling. "Both. Who wants to work this many long days? But I'm serious because I see how the investment in this will save so much time down the road."

"Less after-hours calls."

"Yes!" Charlotte extended a fist bump.

Matt obliged. "Speaking of which, I need to call Allan. We need his purchasing procedure."

"You don't have to call him. We're okay if we don't have it today, Matthew."

"Oooh. You used my full name. You really think I shouldn't call him."

Charlotte shrugged her shoulders. "You're the boss."

"We're only 77% completed with procedures. I really wanted 80 percent before Reggie comes tomorrow."

"Seventy-seven is pretty good. We were at zero percent three months ago." Charlotte closed her laptop and put it in her bag. "Good night, Matt. If you are trying to impress Reggie, I think he will be impressed with what we've achieved." She kissed her brother on the top of the head and left.

Matt watched her walk to the front door and leave. The last three months had been impressive. She had been impressive. They replaced Bob with Kurt and Andrea, and the newbies were already up to veteran speed, surpassing Bob's numbers. On the plus side, they weren't wasting money on unnecessary title work and were generally well-liked. Things were good.

The back door opened. Matt wasn't expecting anyone. He sprang to his feet and rushed out of the conference room and down the dark hallway.

The light shot on. The first thing Matt saw was the mop of blond hair squeezed out beneath a tan Carhartt hat.

"Plumber Stan!"

"Hey Matt!"

Matt looked at the flowers in Stan's hands. "Did Charlotte give you a key?"

"Yes. Is that okay?"

Matt stuttered. "What if you break up? Are you going to give it back?"

A smile gushed across his face. "I don't think we will."

"Oh!"

Plumber Stan's face was puzzled. "Is that okay?"

Matt waved his hands. "She can do what she wants."

"Like give me a key."

"Sure."

Matt motioned to the flowers. "Those are for her, I assume."

"Yes. She's been working really hard. We are meeting in 15 minutes for a late dinner. So I watched for when her car left, and I came to put these in a vase on her desk."

"Those roses are red. That seems serious. And before you ask…yes, it's okay if you two are serious."

"I just wanted her to know that I think she's awesome." Plumber Stan's eyes brightened with dreaminess.

Matt felt the automatic change for Plumber Stan in his heart. "You cherish her, don't you?"

Plumber Stan nodded. "I made her this card." He put the vase down, removed a square of folded yellow construction paper from his pocket, unfolded it, and handed it to Matt. On the front were two stick figures holding hands. One had a skirt, purple hair, and red lips. The other had a hat and brown curls. "I drew yellow curls on the yellow paper, but you couldn't see them. I made my hair brown. My real hair will darken as I get older."

Matt opened the card and read aloud the cartoony font with backward letters.

"Charlotte, Charlotte,
You're my starlet.
Shining bright in my soul.
Your laugh makes me whole.

Charlotte, Charlotte,
My heart bleeds scarlet
because my heart, you stole
and for the Colts in the Super Bowl."

Matt suppressed giggling. "The backward letters are on purpose, like a kid writing it, correct?"

"Yes. I thought it would be cute."

"And the wrong use of 'you're?' You meant y-o-u-r, but that's part of the kid couture?"

Plumber Stan stared blankly at Matt. After an awkward beat, he said, "Yes."

Matt nodded. "And the part about how your heart bleeds for the Colts in the Super Bowl?"

"It's supposed to be funny."

"Okay. I thought so. I didn't want to laugh in case you weren't trying to be funny?"

"To protect my feelings?"

"Yes."

"Thank you. That's very kind."

Matt's heart warmed, and he handed the card back to Plumber Stan. "I think she'll love it. Do you like her purplish hair in real life?"

"Yes. You know, she told me that she is getting back to being her. For the first two years of this business, she said she deformed to being what she had to be for the business—"

Matt's chest twinged. "You mean deformed to what she thought I wanted her to be?"

"Yes. She wants to help you. She always has."

"Do you think you would have fallen for her if you met her with purple hair?"

Plumber Stan shook his head. "No. I'm a simple man. My parents didn't care for her hair at first or the unicorn tattoo on her shoulder. But it's who she is. And I love her."

"You do, don't you?"

"Yes. And if you don't mind, I'm going to put these roses in place and go meet her before I'm late." Plumber Stan started down the hallway.

"Hey, Stan."

"Yes?" Plumber Stan turned around.

"Thanks for loving my sister. You're a great guy."

Plumber Stan's face turned red. "Thanks. She's a great woman."

Matt returned to the conference room and looked at the percentage of completed procedures. "We can get to eighty by tomorrow," he mumbled.

Matt called Allan.

"Yes?" Allan's voice sounded like he had a wall up.

"Reggie is coming tomorrow."

"I know. That's tomorrow. Not tonight."

"You see, Allan, I was wondering if you could get the purchasing SOP done tonight so we can hit an eighty percent completion rate."

Allan sighed long and loud. "It doesn't matter if we have it. You just want to tell Reggie you are at eighty percent."

"But that's our goal, and we are so close."

"I told you I was taking the night off."

"But you said that it was for the final T-ball game. The sun is starting to set. Theodore is not playing right now. He's probably in bed. You knew that we were going to have to work some late nights during this phase."

"No."

"Come on, Allan. It would be so sweet to be at 80 percent."

"Matthew, it will be done by the end of the week, and we will have it for the rest of the company's history."

"Alright," Matt huffed. "Have a great night, Allan."

"Honestly, it won't be now." Allan hung up.

CHAPTER 27

Quarterly Day

Matt walked to the front door for at least the fifth time to see if Reggie had arrived. He had lost count.

"You know, you could just monitor the security cameras," Barb suggested from her cubicle.

"I could." Matt continued to watch the parking lot. "But I have too much energy to sit down."

"Excited?"

"I'm pumped. We're really doing this, Barb! We're at eighty percent of procedures written!"

"Did Allan actually do his last night?" Charlotte popped up from one of the cubicles.

"Stop spying! You don't work in there," Matt complained.

"Eighty percent, Matt?" Charlotte pressed.

"If we round to the nearest ten percent."

Charlotte laughed. "You're cute."

"That's workplace harassment."

Charlotte waved him off. "You're impossible. I'll see you in the conference room."

Matt raised his hands in the air. "I won."

Charlotte didn't respond.

"The Colts are going to win the Super Bowl because someone's heart is controlled? Or something like that."

She turned around, hands on hips. "Now, who's spying?"

"Is it spying if a certain plumber showed it to me when he broke in last night?"

"Broke in?" Charlotte questioned.

"Oh, I'm sorry," Matt mockingly smacked his forehead. "I forgot. You gave him a key."

Charlotte huffed and headed towards the conference room.

"I win again."

A car signaled to turn into the parking lot. Matt felt the rush until he realized it was Allan's car.

Matt's phone buzzed.

Running a little late. – Reggie.

Allan exited his car and closed the door. He stood with his hand on the handle and seemed to sniff the air. He took a deep breath and released it. He muttered something and charged toward the front door.

Matt opened the door for Allan. "Everything okay?"

Allan shrugged.

"Are you mad?"

Allan thought and then shook his head.

"Are you talking today?"

Allan nodded.

"Just not right now?"

Allan continued past Matt.

Matt wanted to stop Allan and make him talk. Instead, he said, "Okay. See you in the meeting in a few." Matt returned to the front windows.

Charlotte whispered behind him, "Who you spying on now?"

"I'm just waiting for Reggie."

"I'm excited, too. We have the processes down."

"Not quite at eighty percent, though."

Charlotte smacked Matt's arm. "Leave him alone. He just wanted to watch Theodore's game."

"He was done with the game. Allan could have gotten us to 80 percent."

"So could we if we had finished another procedure."

"But we don't have another procedure in the hopper. If we did, I would have finished it. Allan just needed to make some adjustments, and —"

"He doesn't have to work every waking moment," Charlotte snapped.

"You're right. He doesn't. Our goal was to have eighty percent done by the time Reggie came."

"I'm happy with what we have."

"I'd be happier if we had eighty."

"Then Allan wouldn't be happy."

"Is 'happy' one of our core values?" Matt asked.

"If you define 'happy' as 'drowning in work.'"

"I'm not like that."

"Leave Allan alone today about it. You just want to impress Reggie."

"No, I don't."

"Yes, you do. Everyone—including you—did an incredible job of getting the policies this far. Allan is overdrawn and strung out, and instead of appreciating him, you communicate that he hasn't done enough."

"I didn't say that!" Matt argued.

"You imply it!" Charlotte snapped.

"You do imply it." Barb's voice wafted over her cubicle.

Matt huffed and charged into the bathroom. He splashed water on his face and wiped it with a towel.

The door opened, and Allan walked in. His red eyes betrayed that he had been crying.

"Are you okay, Allan?"

Allan shrugged.

"Were you crying?"

Allan shrugged again.

"Forget it!" Matt pushed past Allan, exited the bathroom, and ran into Reggie.

"Hey, Matt!" Reggie's cheery voice disturbed Matt's unrest.

Matt stopped and rubbed his temples. "Thanks…thanks for coming."

"Are you okay?

Matt shrugged. "I'm sorry. I'm really glad you are here. Just a rough few minutes. I'll be in the conference room."

Charlotte was already in the conference room when Matt entered. "What do you want me to present to Reggie?" Her tone was cold.

"I don't know. Just whatever he asks, that is your department."

"That's not very helpful."

"I don't care. What's with Allan?"

"I suspect he's worn out, Matt. It's been a good but rough three months."

Matt and Charlotte sat up when Allan and Reggie entered the room. Allan took his usual seat next to Charlotte.

Reggie sat at the head of the table and studied everyone one by one. "This is going to be interesting. I'm reading that the room is tense. But Matt texts me twice a week, and it sounds like progress has been made. Today, we review your goals to see if you've accomplished them, uncover issues, solve issues, and set new goals for the next quarter. If we're good, I will award you an Engagement Day. Judging by the feel in this room, I think we need to start with what's good and what's bad. Matt, what is good?"

"Acquisitions and sales. Since moving on from Bob, we hired Andrea and Kurt. They are killing it because of Charlotte's structure. She's done a great job. So has Allan."

"What's bad?"

"We didn't hit 80 percent completion on our procedures. That was our goal."

Allan released a pent-up sigh.

"Thanks, Matt," Reggie said. "What do you have to say, Charlotte?"

"I think our good is that we are at just under 80% of procedures completed." Charlotte glared at Matt, daring him to object. "It's been a long haul, long hours, but we're at a great place. I think the staff is gelling. There are fewer questions and fewer emergencies. What's bad? Bob resurfaced at Premiere Property Solutions. He didn't go back to selling cars."

"He got a taste of blood and liked it, huh?" Reggie chuckled. "This business is cutthroat."

"I guess so," Charlotte continued. "He beat us on two properties last week. I take it personally. I think about it when I lay in bed. I want to beat him." She looked at her fists as though she hadn't realized she was clenching them. "I don't like being this way."

"Thanks for the transparency," Reggie said.

"I want to beat him, too," Matt said. "Just not as badly as Charlotte. Reggie, I just don't like that Premiere is emerging and taking some properties from us. We didn't meet our quota last week for the first time because we banked on one of those two properties Bob got, and on Friday, it was too late to pivot."

"We'll make it up this week," Charlotte assured.

"Love that attitude, Charlotte," Reggie nodded with admiration. "Allan, it's your turn."

"Good news: We're in a good place. I'm proud of my sister and brother for turning this thing around. Bad news: I'm not the guy to take it to the next level. I'm resigning as CFO."

Allan's words were so soft and sedate that the tone didn't match the action. He couldn't have meant what he just said.

Before Matt could ask for clarification, Charlotte shot to her feet and shrieked, "What? You're leaving us?"

"You're not kidding, are you, Allan?" Matt's entire body felt heavy like he couldn't get out of his chair. "Or are you fooling us? You don't fool around. You're really leaving, aren't you?"

Allan stared at the floor and winced. Charlotte cried, streaking her eye makeup.

Matt thought through possibilities to fix it. "It's my fault, isn't it? We can change some things. Get you help."

Tears dripped from Allan's bowed face. "It's my fault. It's my fault." He choked on his words. "I'm sorry. I'm letting you down."

Matt burst from his chair. "No. We can fix this. We can fix anything."

Charlotte's stare was angry. Matt knew she blamed him. "Sometimes we push things over a cliff, and they crash and shatter and can't be fixed."

Matt knelt and put his hand on Allan's shoulder. "Eighty percent of what we need to do is done."

Allan wiggled away from Matt's hand. He raised his head. "No. My work-life balance is broken."

"But we're almost past the hard part," Charlotte offered. "What would we do without you?"

"Without me?" Allan tapped his chest. "Without me, you would be ahead, and I would be happier?"

"We can make you happy!" Matt insisted.

"I haven't been happy in the two and a half years of doing this. I've been happy to work with you two, but it's just too much for me."

Matt returned to his seat. "I just don't think this is a smart move, Allan."

"May I say something?" Reggie asked. "Building a business is not just about being smart. It's about being healthy. If Allan is not happy and it's negatively affecting him, then this is not healthy."

Matt huffed.

Charlotte sighed. "That is true."

"Allan," Reggie said. "Do you no longer align with the goals and purpose of New Grant City? Is there something different you want the business to be?"

"I align with the goals and purpose of New Grant City. I'm just not in positional alignment."

Reggie nodded. "You're in the wrong seat."

"Exactly!" Alan's response was the most lively he'd been since the meeting started. "And there isn't another seat I want other than the owner's box where I already sit. I'll keep my investment in the business, and I'll invest more if necessary."

"Was there something specific that made you realize this?" Reggie asked.

"Matt is right. He's usually right. He's right about what we need to do. Charlotte is right, too. I'm just not the guy who wants to do it. Last night, Matt called me to see if I would finish a financial procedure, and I didn't do it. I chose to spend time with my kids over the business' needs."

"So you don't plan to get another job, then?" Matt asked.

"Matt, this business is flowing right now. There's a lot of passive income from my investments. I have different ways now that I can care for my family, even the new baby when he comes. I have always been with you on the vision of turning these properties into homes. I never voiced this, but I wanted to get to a point where I was just an owner and not an employee."

"So, you hit some financial metric and are done with us?" Charlotte asked with a tinge of disbelief.

"I'm not done with you," Allan said. "Listen, I put money in this because I believed in Matt and in you. I still do. The passive income doesn't even come close to covering everything I want to do financially."

"Then how will you cover the rest?" Matt asked.

"Matt, how do you think I had the money to invest at start-up? I took my inheritance money and invested it all. I hit on every investment. I'm okay financially. In fact, Lisa and I are thinking about investing more in the company. I'm going to be a fractional CPA, maybe work hard doing some taxes from February through April.

"Another question," Reggie said, "What do you see yourself doing in three years?"

Allan smiled, relieved from the weight that had been lying on him for the past few years. "Help other Matts. Invest in the community. Reggie, I can't tell you how buoyed I am, but what I see NGC becoming. I just can't do this every day. I'm not looking to make a lot of money. I'm looking to have quality time with my kids and help other families. I am not leaving. I'm just not the finance manager anymore. As an owner, I say that we need someone in the seat who would have had the drive to get to 80% last night."

"For the sake of your siblings, can you tell us what seat you see yourself in?"

"The owner's box. Matt even talked about getting the theater and making it a community center. That appeals to me. I might like community service."

"Okay, Allan, none of this is as bad as I first thought." Charlotte grabbed his hand. "I really want you to be happy. And you will be happier with this. And I will help you get this done."

They all looked at Matt.

Matt covered his mouth with his hand as he thought. "Allan, I have nothing but love for you right now. I do feel bad. Like I've been deforming you the past few years. I want you to be happy. Some of this work is even beneath you, but you've been doing it to make this work for us. Thank you."

Reggie clapped his hands together. "Today, we need to build in how to move forward, filling Allan's seat. We need to look at resources and create a succession plan for Allan this quarter. That is part of our strategic plan. But I sense you need a break. This was a lot to take in."

CHAPTER 28

The Glue

Matt poked his head into Charlotte's office. "Breaktime is almost over."

Her back to the door, Charlotte flipped her purple and pink lava lamp.

Matt stepped further in. "You okay?"

"Like you are?" Her voice was scratchy from crying.

"Sadness is just hard for me, Char." Matt closed the door. "Can you turn around?"

Charlotte flipped the lava lamp but didn't turn around. "You can go into that meeting like nothing happened this morning. You can go into that meeting with business as usual. I know."

"I know you can't go in business as usual, Char. Why do you think I came in to talk to you?"

"To tell me that break time was over and it's time to go to work?"

"No."

"That's what you said when you came in."

"Come on. If I walked in here and asked how you were doing, you would say you are okay. WE always dance through this awkward competition. You feel you need to be tough and all business around me and one up me. Then I feel like I have to be right and one-up you."

Charlotte slowly tilted the lava lamp back and forth. "I know you, Matthew. You'll replace Allan with no remorse, no feeling."

Beyond Charlotte, the pictures on her credenza captured Matt's attention. The first was of Allan and Charlotte at her high school graduation. The second was a picture of their family from one Easter Sunday at church.

"Can I tell you what I'm worried about with Allan leaving? It's a mix of several things and probably won't be as emotional as you want, but it will be honest."

Charlotte put the lava lamp down and swiveled around in her chair. Her eyes were red and focused.

"Those two pictures. They worry me."

Charlotte picked up the one of her and Allan at high school graduation.

"That's like a picture with your dad, isn't it?"

She hugged the picture to her chest. "Yes. That's why losing him sucks."

"But the other picture…do you remember that day?"

"No." Charlotte swapped pictures and placed it between them where she and Matt could both see it.

Matt pointed to himself on the far left. "It was taken my junior year of high school, four to five years before Mom and Dad died. I put on that off-white Abercrombie and Fitch shirt and tan jeans to annoy them. Everyone's outfit was colorful. They told me I couldn't wear my outfit to church, especially because it was Easter. I waited to come out to the car until I knew there was no time left for them to send me back in because they didn't want to be late."

"Always a jerk!" Charlotte punched his arm.

"I chose the shirt with the largest 'AF' I had."

"Is that why you are smiling so big?"

Matt frowned. "Yes. It's a smile of pride and arrogance. I was a teenage boy who had won against his family."

"At least everyone's happy in the picture, the way Mom and Dad and Allan have their arms around each other. Maybe that's why I like it."

"Mom and Dad had joy. I could never ruin their day. I love you in this picture, Char. Third grade. Pink bunny ears. The way you're leaning forward with your basket, as though you are offering candy to the photographer. The pink and blue and purple of your dress. It's so you."

"Everyone is hugging except you," Charlotte noted. "You almost look like a photobomber invading this loving family."

Matt laughed. "Rebellious phase. I was more like an intruder. But look at Allan. His right hand is starting to extend towards me like he wanted to pull me in."

"It looks slightly awkward with Allan trying to be in the family hug and reaching for you. But that's our brother! He wants to keep the family together."

Matt studied Allan in the picture. "Man, he was gangly. That gray suit was the only one he had. His arms are too long for the suit."

"Mom and Dad probably couldn't afford another one."

"That's what I thought until we got an inheritance. They were saving it up for us later in life. That silly blue and purple and pink bubbly tie was a poor match for the gray suit. And I tried to embarrass him for it."

"Sounds like something you would have done, Matt."

"I tried. We were waiting to have our pictures taken after church, so a group of teens found each other and were talking. You wandered over and annoyed me just by being present. This was when Allan and Lisa first had a thing going. To get some laughs, I made fun of Allan's sleeves and his tie. Most of the kids laughed. Lisa didn't."

"What did Allan do?"

"He straightened up and said, 'I picked this tie because Charlotte wanted someone to match her.' And then you threw your arms around his waist and hugged him."

"Awww," Charlotte gushed as a tear dripped from her eye.

"And a few minutes later, he was trying to pull me into the family hug even though I had been trying to embarrass him in front of my friends and the girl he liked. He has always been the family glue." Matt sat back in the chair. His instinct was to wipe the tear from his eye and pretend like it was never there. Instead, he and Charlotte locked eyes and smiled as more tears flowed.

"Here's what worries me," Matt continued. "He's leaving. Allan is right. This isn't the job for him. Allan brought you into this business when I didn't want you. You and I need our own glue. We might never have pictures of just the two of us on our desks, but I want you to know that I want you here. We wouldn't be where we are without you. You are brilliant, and you connect with everyone in this office better than I do. You bring something to New Grant City that I could never offer. Now then, can we end this emotional nightmare of a moment for me?"

Charlotte laughed. "Not yet." She rose from her seat, and Matt did the same. She hugged her brother tightly.

"Hey!" Allan called.

They both looked up.

Allan snapped a picture. "Just trying to commemorate a few things here."

"Sheesh. Did you get me crying?" Matt asked.

"I hope so!" Charlotte picked up her laptop and exited her office. "Time to meet."

CHAPTER 29

The FOCUS

"You can have more time if you need it," Reggie said when the siblings entered the conference room.

"I think we're good," Matt said.

"I'm really good!" Allan sang and danced over to his seat.

Charlotte laughed.

"I'm happy that you are happy, bro," Matt said.

"I am. I feel free. I feel like a weight is off my chest."

"So…about that more money you were going to invest."

"I just said that to appease you in the moment," Allan said.

Matt's face dropped. "Okay. I get that."

"I'm just kidding!" The words burst from Allan's mouth, and he laughed.

"I think I like stressed Allan better," Matt said. "Let's get started, Reggie!"

Reggie rubbed his hands together like he was a chef excited to create a new dish.

"We have already done introductions, so let's do Core Values Violations. Remember this agenda is on page 56 of the RISE Curriculum. What are your Core Values?

Charlotte answered, "Belief, Respect, Integrity, Drive, Generosity."

"I thought Drive was first," Matt protested.

"I rearranged them so it's like 'bridge' but with no 'e' on the end."

"Should we add an 'e' value?" Matt asked. "Like empathetic."

Charlotte rolled her eyes.

"Obviously, I was joking, Char."

Reggie laughed and shook his head. "You guys crack me up. I used you as an example at a coaching session I did."

"For our humor and ability to get along?" Matt asked.

"Sort of," Reggie said. "It's for your transparency. There's no holding back with you guys. You say what needs to be said, and then you say even more. No one hides anything. You say you are sorry when necessary. You hug and make up. And from what Matt said in recent texts, you guys are rising with the RISE curriculum."

"I'd agree," Charlotte said.

"So, are there any Core Values violations?" Reggie asked.

"Yes. Respect." Matt offered.

Reggie raised his eyebrows. "Tell us more."

"I didn't respect Allan's home life. I'm sorry."

Allan's eyes widened. "Thank you, Matt. That means a lot."

"Anyone else?" Reggie pointed at each sibling, giving them a chance to answer.

No one did.

"Next is purpose alignment. Have you identified any products or partnerships over the past week that misalign with your stated purpose? You three have anything?"

Everyone shook their head.

"Then I'm throwing the penalty flag and giving you a Reggie Singer Stinger."

"Ouch!" Matt sat up in his chair.

"In my conversations with Matt, I think there is something that is off. I was waiting until today to bring it up, hoping that one of you three would notice."

Matt looked for an answer from Charlotte and Allan. They merely shrugged. "No idea, Reggie."

"Why are you pursuing the theater?"

"Double ouch!" Charlotte winced.

"What's wrong with the theater?" Matt protested. "The city announced that they are taking offers for the property. Our neighborhoods need a community center."

"They probably do need one, but what does that have to do with the purpose of NGC? Isn't your purpose to put five thousand families into homes in ten years?"

"Yes!"

"Are you converting those sloped theater floors into housing? Are people going to roll out of bed and down to the front door?"

"It's a dream of Matt's because of the shooting and James Burks," Charlotte said.

"Charlotte, it's an incredible, worthy, honorable, compassionate dream. But is the purpose of NGC to build a community center?"

The room was silent.

"It's my dream," Matt said. "Not theirs."

"How would we incorporate it, Reggie?" Allan asked. "Could we make it part of our purpose?"

Reggie exhaled long and slow like a person trying to be calm. "Can I be cold for a minute?"

"Are you mad at us?" Matt asked.

"No."

"Go ahead and be cold for a minute, Reggie." Matt smiled. "Go ahead."

"You have to FOCUS. That's an acronym. Follow One Course Until Successful. For a minute, can you imagine you aren't a family working together?"

"Allan can because he actually quit today." Matt laughed at his own joke.

Reggie grimaced. "It's been a stressful day for you. I'll let that bad joke go without pointing out how bad it was."

"I can do that, Reggie," Charlotte said.

"Thanks. NGC is not here to fulfill Matt's dreams. We are here to turn NGC into an efficient beast that will financially allow you to fulfill your other dreams. NGC is about real estate and tenants and flips. Spending capital on a side dream is not what you want to do at this point."

Matt's face fell. "I hear what you are saying, Reggie. I get it."

"Now, Matt, your dream was to start this business and be your own boss. I think you wanted to be a leader and not a dictator, if I remember correctly."

"Correct."

"Let's follow that dream for now," Reggie said. "Can we all agree to that?"

"I'm not sure," Allan said.

Matt's jaw dropped. "You're the last person in this room, I figured would say that."

"I mean, that's the neighborhood we grew up in, Reggie. I think part of Matt's motivation in starting NGC was redeeming James Burks' murder."

Reggie held out his hands. "I understand that, Allan. But then you need to start a not-for-profit and apply the same RISE business standards to that. The purpose of NGC's business dealings is not to redeem James' death. The purpose of NGC's business dealings is not to honor your parents."

"Ouch!" Charlotte winced.

"Charlotte, I'm not trying to hurt you," Reggie said. "The purpose of NGC's business dealings is to put 5,000 families into homes. You FOCUS on that. Follow One Course Until Successful. Buying an old theater to convert into a community center is just diverting you from rising as NGC."

Matt said, "I think I get what you are saying, Reggie. I don't think he's trying to hurt us, Charlotte. This is right up my alley because we need to divorce our feelings from it. We all have a heart for Grant City because of our upbringing. But what if we had started our business in Gary or South Bend? Would NGC be trying to buy a theater to convert into a community center?"

"Great point!" Reggie cheered.

"No. We wouldn't be trying to get a community center," Charlotte said. "But I really want this for you, Matt. The closing date for offers is not too far off. There's only one unique building in front of which James was killed as he walked next to you. There's only one theater where the police continually clear out junkies like the one who killed our parents."

"Listen to me," Reggie pleaded. "You are doing great as NGC. Allan moving out of the CFO seat and strictly into an owner's seat is great for NGC. You are becoming a strong, lean machine. There will be future days when you can be generous. But you're not at that stage yet."

"Reggie, Can we move past this for now?" Matt asked. "Between Allan leaving his CFO seat and shutting down the community center dream, this is a really heavy morning. I agree that these are good moves, though. I understand how this is purpose alignment."

"We can do that," Reggie assured. "Let's move on to the Key Profit Indicators. What do you have, Allan?"

Matt mentally checked out. Exhaustion suffocated his attention on the conversation. Charlotte's lips were drawn tight like they were when she wanted to object. Matt texted her.

"*Maybe if we hit it hard these next three months, we'd have the $$$???*"

Charlotte read the text and pulled her phone to her lap so she could type under the table.

"*Rebel! You are losing FOCUS, Matt!* ☺"

Matt smirked as Reggie and Allan continued to talk. He typed his text under the table.

"*Reggie is right. He's looking out for us. But I think that we could have cash on hand to do it. It can be our short-term goal.*"

Charlotte read the text and caught Matt's gaze. She subtly nodded and then shook her head.

"*I just don't know, Matt.*"

"Okay, let's do Resource Audit," Reggie said. "Seems like there's a glaring resource need with the opening of the CFO seat. Part of the strategic plan is to create a succession plan for Allan this quarter. How long do you plan to stay in the seat, Allan?"

"I'd like to leave as soon as possible but not hurt Matt and Charlotte."

"We also could use a Project Manager and a Sales Manager," Matt said.

"I know who we could get to be the Project Manager," Allan sang and smirked.

Matt laughed, "Are you high?"

Allan's eyebrows narrowed as he looked at Charlotte. "I'm thinking of someone who is high on love: Plumber Stan."

"Oooh. Plumber Stan," Matt said. "If this works out with Charlotte, then it could be more of a family operation."

"I think Plumber Stan is trying to date his way to the top of NGC," Allan teased.

"Allan! Stop it. I expect that from Matt," Charlotte complained.

"I just like being a free man," Allan said. "It feels good acting like you two and saying whatever I want."

Matt laughed. "I like Free Allan. Maybe I should start calling you 'Free Allan' like we call our potential project manager 'Plumber Stan.'"

Charlotte sighed. "You know, I have been meaning to explain to you two boys that 'Plumber' is not on his birth certificate."

"You got under her skin, Allan. It's kind of fun, isn't it?" Matt asked.

Allan tilted his head one way and then the other and shrugged.

Reggie busted out laughing. "You guys are entertaining. Let's get back to Inspiration. How are you doing on Inspiration? Are you inspiring your team through personal interactions and the emotional paycheck?"

Matt said, "A few weeks ago, we had a Four-Day Weekend contest. We had an ambitious goal for a total number of deals agreed to, and deals closed in a one-week period. If we hit it, we would have Monday and Tuesday off the following week. And we hit it by Thursday!"

Charlotte bubbled, "And we beat Bob on three of the agreements! That was my emotional paycheck!"

"And Matt still made us come into work on Friday even though we had hit the goal," Allan complained.

"But did you actually work that day? I recall you encouraging people to take long breaks by showing them photo albums on your phone of my niece and nephew."

Allan replied, "I was silently protesting having to come in!"

"So the four-day weekend and beating Bob sounds like an emotional paycheck!" Reggie opined. "Tell me how Systems are doing? What's working? What's not and needs to be retooled?"

Charlotte answered, "Ever since we started tracking the Key Process Indicators—"

"And fired Bob!" Allan added. "Don't forget that Matt fired Bob then."

Charlotte sneered at no one in particular. "I don't like talking about when Bob was here. But ever since then, Reggie, we have tracked the processes and we have found that emails have worked best for us. We hired another virtual assistant just for emails."

"What about an Engagement audit? I think we are at a point where I will award you an Engagement Day. What marketing channels need to be adjusted or retooled?"

Matt and Charlotte looked blankly at each other.

"We don't know," Matt finally said.

"Then let's do the RISE assessment for Engagement on page 4 of the workbook. Question one: On a scale of one to three, do you have a logo, brand guide, and consistent digital presence that keeps you top-of-mind with customers?"

"Ooooh!" Charlotte said. "I'd love to go back and see what I initially answered for this. We have a logo."

"I think we have a brand guide," Matt said. "I like the way things look."

"We don't really have one, Matt," Charlotte admitted. "I have played with the colors and fonts and design."

"What do you think, Allan?" Reggie asked.

"I don't pay attention to it," Allan said.

"I'd give us a two," Matt said.

"It's the low side of two," Charlotte said. "I take the blame. I've focused so much on systems."

"Don't be too hard on yourself," Reggie said. "You're almost there. Get these processes done and you'll conquer engagement. And then you'll be ready to coach people yourself."

"Me?" Matt asked.

Reggie laughed. "Sorry I laughed so hard. No, not you. Charlotte?"

"Me?" Charlotte asked.

"Absolutely," Reggie said.

Allan put his feet on the table and leaned back. "I've thought that since we started." He looked at Matt. "You're probably going to lose her, too."

"No way!" Matt protested. "Never."

"I'm just saying that she has the talent to notice what is wrong," Reggie said, "the communication skills to explain it, and the gentleness to deal with big personalities, and the fire to put people in their place if she needs to."

"Gentleness. And you thought he was talking about you, Matt?" Allan chided.

"Whatever, Allan. You quit, and now you have jokes."

"How about we do question two?" Reggie asked. "Do you have consistent company messaging that carries through to all of your marketing materials and creative?"

"Definitely," Matt said. "We use 'Building Grant City by putting families into homes' on all of our materials."

"It's on our email signatures," Allan added.

"It's a three," Matt said.

"No," Charlotte said. "I have been thinking about incorporating the Core Values into some of our materials. I don't think people really know what we are about. Sometimes I wonder if having Grant City in our name gets lost in us doing business in Grant City."

"Anything else?"

"I'm not sure where this fits in," Charlotte added, "but I don't think we are well known as Bob. Bob sold cars for a lot of years in this city. He knows a lot of people. He talks to a lot of people. He's been a pain in the butt since he left."

"That ties into the next question. Do you have effective advertising channels that are measured weekly and adjusted when proven ineffective?

You can't have the experience and networking that Bob has if you don't have Bob. But you can advertise."

"Yes, because we've been moving more towards emails," Charlotte answered.

"But you need to keep monitoring it," Reggie warned. "It might change a week from now."

"I've seen it for many weeks from the key process indicators. Emails are still working for us. It's not like I noticed it four weeks ago and haven't measured since."

Reggie winked at her. "That's the way you do it. And be prepared to shift as necessary. The last question is this: do you have a proven sales process, weekly training, and measurable success turning leads into paying customers?"

"We're probably a 2 on that," Matt said. "As we said, we need a sales manager. I think we actually did learn a few things from Bob that we have implemented."

"I think we have really learned how to have a lot of lines in the water, but we can't reel them all in," Allan added. "The Sales Manager is a great idea."

"So let me sum this up," Reggie said. "You are having success, but not greater success because you're not as well-known as Bob, and you have average but not great engagement with customers."

"Yes!" Matt said.

"Definitely!" Charlotte said.

"I don't know. That was never my area." Allan put his feet back up on the conference room table and leaned back.

Reggie chuckled. "Then I think the next thing is to schedule an Engagement Day in three months when you do your next quarterly strategy session."

"Awesome!" Matt said. "Charlotte will schedule it with you."

CHAPTER 30

The Broken Dream

"No. No. No. Matt, just stop." Charlotte's face tightened. "We are not bidding on the theater. I've wanted to, but we can't lose focus. Things are going so well. Reggie is coming tomorrow. Remember how much you wanted to impress him last time he came? He won't be impressed if you win the bid for the theater."

"This is the last day for bids. They announce the winner tomorrow morning at 11! It's been a great quarter."

"We cannot spend our capital on that. Do you think if Allan were here that he would agree?"

"Char, someone is going to buy my dream. It's eating me."

"What is eating you? That Bob might buy it. That he sent you emails bragging that nobody was topping their bid?"

"But you weren't this close to death in front of that building. It's the vision, Char. It's the big picture."

"No, it's not the big picture. The big picture is putting five thousand families into homes, Matthew."

"This is the bigger picture, then."

"Matt, forget for a moment that you will hurt our momentum by tying up capital in the theater. What will tomorrow be like when Reggie is in the middle of Engagement Day, and you announce that you won a bid for a building that has nothing to do with our focus? By the way, the last time Reggie was here, he told you not to buy it."

Matt's phone buzzed. It was a text from Reggie.

"Don't bid on the theater. - Reggie"

Matt gasped and pointed at Charlotte. "You're a snitch!"

"What?" Charlotte pulled at her hair.

"Reggie texted me and said that I shouldn't bid on the theater."

"I didn't tell Reggie!"

"Does he have this place bugged? Under surveillance? Or does he have a mole?" Matt raised his eyebrows at Charlotte.

"You are beyond lunacy right now.

Matt's phone buzzed again with a text from Reggie.

"Buying the theater doesn't fulfill your purpose."

"Ugh! This might be worse than Bob's taunting texts about the theater."

"Why don't you just block Bob on your phone?"

"He drives me, Charlotte."

"Matt, he's driving you crazy. I can't stand Bob. I'm glad he's gone. I don't want to lose anything to him. But if you get off course, what is that going to say to everyone who works here?"

Matt huffed and turned his back to Charlotte.

The phone buzzed with a third text from Reggie.

"You will lose by buying the theater."

The phone buzzed again. This time, it was a text from Bob.

Matt gasped. "Charlotte, Bob sent me a picture of a cleared city lot, and his text says, 'Future picture of your theater before we replace it with a strip mall.'"

"Matt, he's just taunting you. What you think will be a victory will be a loss. There will be so many more opportunities to help Grant—"

Matt hurled his phone across his office, shattering it against the wall.

"What in the world, Matt?"

Matt marched out of his office.

Charlotte followed him. "Where are you going?"

"To get a new phone."

"You might need your SIM card."

Matt marched back into the office and picked up the remnants of the phone.

"Thank you." He looked at his sister, whose eyes were wide. "In case you're wondering, I do feel better now. If I can't buy a theater, I think I'll buy myself one of those phones that folds, and even the screen folds. And it will be a few hours until I can read another text from Bob. So this is good."

Charlotte frowned.

Matt loudly exhaled. "I'll be okay, Char. Everyone's right. I don't need to buy the theater. I'm just going to take the rest of the day off."

"You're not going to the government center to make a bid, are you?"

"No. I'm really not. I just want to be alone and mourn a little."

When he got in his car, Matt's impulse was to put his phone in the holder. He tossed the broken phone onto the passenger's seat. Matt pulled out of the parking lot with the intention of making a right and heading to the cell phone store, but he found peace in knowing that Reggie, Bob, Allan, and Charlotte couldn't text him. But what if Jean needed him?

Matt turned left onto Broadway and headed towards the neighborhoods where NGC did much of their work. Within two miles, the streets were dingier with litter in the gutters. At a stoplight, two souped-up cars competed to have the most volume and bass. The bus shelter glass had been shattered and lay scattered on the sidewalk. Fresh graffiti covered the sign that once read "City Hall" and pointed to the left. On the right was the small stadium of a failed Rookie League team for the

Reds. Viny weeds covered some of the graffiti on the exterior brick wall. Wrigley Field it was not.

The light changed, and the two souped-up cars spun out. One screeched to a stop before it would have hit an oblivious jaywalker who was wrapped up in his headphones. Matt automatically thought of his parents being hit and killed in a car accident. For the last fourteen years, he thought about them every time he saw a fender bender or slammed on his brakes.

As Matt stopped at the next light, he noticed that the chain link fence around an abandoned park had broken away from its poles and flopped over the sidewalk. Part of him wondered if anyone would ever fix it.

Something caught his eye in the park. The city was building a cement curb. The site looked as though the city was revitalizing the curb that used to be around the Hub Playground. There was no equipment there anymore, just a grown-over area that once housed monkey bars and swings and metal slides that burned your butt on a summer day.

Matt changed course, turned right, made another right, and parked on the other side of the park. The city was turning up the dirt and reseeding the turf on this end of the park. NGC had revitalized the townhouses across from the park. The twelve attached units were clean and manicured. Five of them had vibrant flowers potted on the stoops and balconies. Two women with strollers talked in front of one of them. A driver darted from an Amazon delivery van and left a package at one of the doors.

Matt returned to Broadway. The theater was up on the left. Matt turned onto a side street and parked near Mrs. Burks' house. He walked to the corner and crossed back over Broadway. In the lot across the intersection and diagonal to the theater, a giant sign showed Bob's face and read, "Premier Property Solutions presents Kroger Grocery and Pharmacy." The next line read, "Coming Next Summer."

If Matt had a BB gun, he would have shot the eyes out of the sign.

A wave of nausea crashed through his body. How could he think such a thing as he stood on this sidewalk? It was the same sidewalk from which a gang member shot into the crowd as it left the theater across the street seventeen years earlier.

When James died.

Matt replayed the night again in his mind. The questions bombarded him.

What if he was walking where James walked?

What if they had decided to go back to James' house and had been walking the other way?

What if they were a little slower?

What if they were a step quicker?

What if they had stayed to watch the credits or even movie hopped?

"That building's not bringing James back!"

Matt immediately knew that the voice belonged to Mrs. Burks. Ashamed of the tears in his eyes, he didn't want to turn and look at her.

"The auction is over today. The building will be awarded tomorrow."

"You know what, Matthew Wellington? I know that. I've read that sign every day when I walk by. Bids are due in city hall by 2 p.m. today. You want it, don't you?"

Matt nodded.

"What for?"

Matt sighed. "Redemption? History? It's personal? See that guy over there?" He pointed at Bob's picture. "He thinks he's going to get it. He'll probably tear it down and put a Dollar General or 7-11 gas station there."

"Good!" Mrs. Burks exclaimed.

"Good? What?" Matt finally looked at her.

"Matthew, that man over there is doing good for us." She pointed to the sign.

"He's not a nice man."

She shrugged. "Maybe not, but do you know how long it's been since we've had a pharmacy around here? You probably have four within two miles of where you live."

"I think there are only three."

Mrs. Burks laughed. "And we get a big supermarket right here! I don't have to get on the bus to shop and limit myself to the groceries I can carry. I'm going to buy my own shopping cart and roll it down to the Kroger and back to my house. I'm going to paint it electric blue so no one thinks I took it from a store."

It was Matt's turn to laugh. "I can picture that."

"Matthew, do you know why that Kroger is coming?"

"Because Bob is dabbling in commercial?"

She slapped his arm. "I don't even know what you are talking about. Kroger is coming because of you and Allan and Charlotte."

"What?"

"You fixed up those houses on my block. You three have fixed up lots of blocks in these past few years. And I don't know what happened to you three the past nine months, but I see NGC signs on properties all over the place. You three mean business. It's like you took that Chicago shark business sense and brought it here. If people weren't moving back in, Kroger wouldn't be building right there. The city wouldn't be fixing the Hub Playground. You rebuilt those townhouses. You did, Matthew. That's some serious tax revenue for the city. Those people are demanding a park for their kids. Look, no one cares if it's because of you or because of Bald Bob on that sign over there. They just want a better place to live."

"Thank you, Mrs. Burks."

"I wasn't done talking! People don't care who is doing it. But I know who is doing it. I know who started it. So, on behalf of me, James, and everyone else, I say, 'Thank you.' You don't need your face on a sign. You don't have to redeem that theater. You are already part of redeeming us and the neighborhood."

Mrs. Burks threw her arms around Matt and squeezed him.

The dam burst. Matt sobbed, pouring tears onto Mrs. Burks' coat. They weren't tears of sadness, but tears of satisfaction and accomplishment, but he also cried because he knew he was saying farewell to the theater. Reggie was right. The theater wasn't part of his FOCUS. Seeing the park and the townhouses and hearing Mrs. Burks' words had convinced him that he didn't need the theater.

"Are you going to be okay?"

"It's been an emotional day. I don't do well with emotions."

"Do you want to come over for a cup of coffee?"

"Thank you, but no. I have to go get a new cell phone."

CHAPTER 31

Engagement Day

Matt felt surprisingly focused the next morning. It was Engagement Day. It was supposed to be Theater Day, but it truly didn't matter. He had already received three texts from Bob. Matt hadn't read them. He didn't want to see Bob's taunts.

Matt sent Bob a voice-to-text.

"Congratulations on the theater! And congratulations on Kroger. It means a lot to the community."

Sending the text didn't feel as good as Matt hoped it would. He needed a little cheering up.

Reggie and Charlotte entered the conference room.

"Engagement Day!" Reggie said as he settled into his seat at the head of the table and began setting himself up for the day. "What a journey it's been."

Charlotte scrutinized her brother.

"I'm fine," Matt mouthed.

Charlotte's lips tightened with skepticism.

"Let's get into Engagement Day," Reggie said.

"And we start with something positive," Charlotte said.

"We always start with something positive," Reggie beamed. "See, you can be a coach, Charlotte."

"I'll start," Charlotte said. "The last three months have been unreal. Systems creation has freed up so much time. We've hired five more people. At this rate, we are going to hit our 5,000 homes goal in less than ten years. Allan sounds happy when we talk. That means so much to me. How about you, Reggie?"

"What's positive for me? I don't think anyone's ever asked me that in a meeting." Reggie pondered for a moment. "In the past three months, I had my first grandchild. My daughter is a mom. That little girl of mine is a mom! I can't believe it. My wife and I have been talking about me cutting back a little, and I'm at peace with that. Maybe staying more local and not as many trips away. My son just re-enlisted in the Army. I'm proud of him. My second youngest got accepted to NYU. My youngest son just turned ten."

Charlotte raised her eyebrows. "You have a ten-year-old son?"

Reggie chuckled. "So, you're saying I'm too old for that?"

Charlotte patted Reggie's hand. "I'm just surprised."

"So were we when we found out Adelia was pregnant almost eleven years ago. I do feel a little too old to be raising a son. Especially since he's an athlete."

"Is that why you're thinking about cutting back?" Charlotte asked.

"Part of it. It's the right decision for us. We are finally in a position to do some things we've always thought of doing."

"That's awesome!" Charlotte said.

"I talk about taking fewer trips, but these trips to coach you have been worthwhile. You'd be surprised how many people want coaching, but don't implement the plan. By helping you, I help Grant City. You two are worth the investment."

Charlotte blushed. "Thank you, Reggie."

"How about you, Matt?" Reggie asked. "What's positive?"

Matt twiddled his thumbs. "A lot. Yesterday, I realized that you were right about the theater. The reason I didn't bid was not because people opposed it. I didn't bid because it was the right decision. I ran into one of our tenants, and she raved about how we've been helping the neighborhoods. Yesterday, I saw some evidence of it. The theater will get sold. It will likely get torn down, and that's okay. Maybe it needs to be torn down."

Reggie groaned. "That's deep. Sounds healthy. I've talked to Charlotte a few times this quarter. I got the impression that with her focusing on hiring salespeople, you were chasing squirrels."

"I wanted to, but I came to the conclusion that I'm not a hunter."

"Matt, I don't blame you for wanting the theater. You're a visionary with his vision a little too far ahead of his current position."

"Out in front of my skis?"

"Maybe, but that's what makes a great visionary sometimes."

"Jean was willing to mortgage the house to buy it if I wanted to. I thought about taking her up on it. But that's one time I thought, 'Matt, you are too obsessed with this.'"

"I kind of wanted the building," Charlotte said.

"Why is that?" Reggie asked.

"I want to crush Bob."

Matt and Reggie laughed.

"I didn't really want to crush Bob," Matt said. "I wanted the building long before Bob came back into this picture."

"I don't really care about the building like you, Matt," Charlotte confessed. "I hurt for you. I know how much it means to you."

"Thanks, Char!"

"So, what's not working?" Reggie asked.

"We need a bigger brand," Matt said. "If we had more money, more deals, more customers, and we were better known, then we could have the money for the community center."

"Thanks, Matt! What do you think, Charlotte?" Reggie asked.

"Reggie, I agree with Matt. I feel like the two of us have taken Resources, Inspiration, and Systems and run with it. I feel like we're ready to grow bigger. The only reason things aren't working is because we haven't learned to make them work yet."

"Then are you ready to work on Engagement?" Reggie asked.

"Yes!" Charlotte said.

"I'm ready for Charlotte to work on it," Matt teased.

Reggie said, "Here are the things we are going to have done by the end of the day: your brand logo, colors, design, marketing message, how we say what we say, who we are, advertising channels, and training and tools for your salespeople. Are you hiring a sales manager?"

"Yes," Charlotte said. "I think we have identified her. I'm trying to iron out the details. Once she's onboarded, it will free me up for engagement."

"And eventually, you will need a Chief Marketing Officer, won't you?" Reggie winked.

"If we keep growing as we are!"

"You've replaced Allan?" Reggie asked.

"Yes," Charlotte answered. "We hired his assistant, Aaliyah. She's got a year left of college. She decided to go online and be around for her dad, who is struggling with health."

"I don't like her," Matt joked. "She is always telling me that I did something wrong. Which I guess means that she's doing her job."

Charlotte pointed to herself. "Remember that you hired someone else who hadn't finished college yet. Look at how that has worked out."

"And you still haven't finished college," Matt added.

"Do I need to at this point?" Charlotte asked.

Matt pointed at himself. "Not as long as you have me as the visionary of this operation."

Charlotte nodded, "Fair enough."

"When we are done today," Reggie said, "you will have a plan for getting out your message. Charlotte, tell me your ideas for branding."

As soon as Charlotte started speaking, Matt zoned out. The next two-plus hours passed in a haze. Engagement was really Charlotte's niche. Matt had been amazed by her growth with systems. Engagement was more natural to her. He had become the Inspiration guy at NGC, finding ways to keep people excited about the dream and write emotional paychecks.

Matt offered little input, agreeing every time he was asked for an opinion. The emotions from the previous day still wore him out. His brain had checked out of the conference room.

At 10:35, Matt looked at the time on his phone. The theater would be awarded within 30 minutes. Matt closed his eyes to take one last trip through his dream. He imagined walking into the large lobby, the theater to the left for organizations to hold seminars or churches to meet during the week. The balcony would be converted into a second level with a basketball court and space for classrooms and hanging out and after-school programs that offered tutoring, introduced teens to careers, and prepared them for success.

"It's not my FOCUS, right?" Matt blurted out his thoughts.

"What?" Charlotte asked.

"No, it's not," Reggie said without missing a beat. "I've been wondering where your head is. Now I know. Let's take five and then head out for an early lunch. We need to clear our heads."

"Sounds good," Matt said.

"But I want to say something first," Reggie continued. "Charlotte, I think it's a good thing you were here to lead the business through this and keep the company focused. With Allan leaving and Matt a little unfocused lately, you have done a great job. You're a leader and a coach."

"No! No, she's not! You're not taking her. You said this the last time she was here." Matt said.

"I'm not trying to take her for RISE. She can really help businesses. As you get in better shape at NGC and she thinks about her future, she might find that she loves coaching and wants to do a little of it."

"Honestly, I haven't thought about it since last time," Charlotte said.

"That might be because you've been so busy coaching here," Reggie said. "I just know that I see the ability in you."

She sheepishly shrugged. "I might be interested in helping the other Matts out there."

"You are so completely not interested in doing that and leaving me," Matt insisted.

Reggie shook his head. "Just be at my rental car at 10:45."

CHAPTER 32

The New Foundation

At 10:45, Reggie pulled out of his parking spot with Charlotte as the co-pilot and Matt sitting in the back seat.

"The nice lunch areas are to the right," Charlotte said.

Reggie made a left. "I might drive around a little. It's still a little early. I just felt like we needed to get out of the office."

Matt leaned against the door, closed his eyes, and put his feet up on the back seat. It felt nice to not have to be in control and just let Reggie drive. Matt fought drifting off to sleep as he listened to the small talk from the front seat.

As they came to a stop, Charlotte asked, "What kind of food do you want, Reggie?"

"Barbecue? Seafood? Steak? Doesn't matter. I'm treating."

"You're not treating!" Matt opened his eyes and noticed the defaced city hall sign and the bus shelter with the broken glass on Broadway. "Where are we going?"

"Just driving around. Slowly. I'm getting older," Reggie said.

"You're not going over to the theater, are you?" Matt asked.

Reggie shrugged.

Matt swung his feet onto the floor. "What are we doing?"

"Maybe you need to have an exorcism on the site right at 11:00," Charlotte suggested.

"Do you know what we are doing, Char?" Matt asked.

"I got in this car thinking that we were going to an early lunch. So, no."

"Wow! Do you see how big Bob's head is on that sign?" Charlotte asked as they approached the intersection of the theater and the new Kroger.

"Look!" Matt pointed at the theater. "There's a news camera there."

"A lot of people," Reggie said. "Street is closed. I'm going to find a place to park."

"Do you know what's going on?" Matt asked.

Reggie shook his head.

"I don't believe you, Reggie," Matt said.

"Matt, I live in the New York City tri-state area. You live somewhere between Chicago, Indianapolis, and Lake Michigan. I don't know these streets. I made a left out of your parking lot and have been driving straight on this road. But now that we are here let's see what's going on."

Reggie parked on a side street.

"I'm intrigued," Charlotte admitted.

"I feel like you're trying to traumatize me," Matt said.

"You said that you were fine about not getting the theater," Reggie said. "Why would this traumatize you?"

They got out of the car and passed through the barricades that closed Broadway. The sidewalks along this stretch were wide, accommodating the people who used to flood out of the theater. The space on the sidewalks and in the street was needed for the assembling crowd. A podium with the seal of Grant City and an Indiana state flag was set up.

"Let's go get on TV." Charlotte grabbed Matt's hand and pulled him behind the reporter. "It's FOX57."

Matt and Charlotte pushed their way behind the male reporter, who wore a FOX57 polo.

The camera light turned red. Charlotte waved at the camera from her spot behind the reporter.

"Might as well make this fun," Matt whispered to his sister. He plastered a cheesy smile on his face and waved.

"We're coming to you from Grant City," the reporter said, "a city that Governor Reynolds recently recognized as a revitalization zone. Seventeen years ago, a Mr. Basketball finalist, James Burks, was shot and killed in front of this very theater, caught in the crossfire of two gangs and cutting short a potential college basketball career. Many city residents point to this event as the straw that broke the camel's back and ushered in the degradation of these central city neighborhoods. Today, Governor Reynolds, along with Mayor Selena Juarez, will announce who won the rights to this theater as part of the Revitalize Indiana campaign."

The camera turned off. The crowd grew into the closed street. Matt and Charlotte moved closer to the stage.

"Huh. Publicity stunt for Governor Reynolds," Matt said to Charlotte.

"It's probably good for his re-election," Charlotte offered.

"It's like RISE's Engagement, but with politics." Matt looked around for Reggie but couldn't see him in the growing sea of people who were starting to crowd the street. Some lifted re-election signs for Governor Reynolds. A few signs touted him for the next presidential election. One person hoisted a "Preserve the Theater" sign. Another held a "For James Burks sign."

"Wow! I thought this would be announced via an email to the bidders," Charlotte said.

"Me, too," Matt agreed.

Charlotte pulled Matt close to her. "Did you bid, Matthew?"

"No," he leaned over and said in her ear.

Several police officers hustled the governor and mayor onto the platform. The crowd mostly applauded. A few booed, but the supporters responded with louder cheers.

"Is Bob going to get to meet the governor?" Charlotte asked.

Matt shrugged.

The governor gave a short speech about his Revitalize Indiana campaign. He touted its success and how Kroger coming back into this neighborhood was proof. Mayor Juarez took the podium when he was done. Her speech was less polished but folksier, thanking those whose vision was improving the city.

"Now it's time to announce the winning offer. We received many offers and took many factors into account. With the Revitalize Indiana campaign in mind, we accepted an offer that stays true to the original purpose of having this theater in this neighborhood. We award the theater to…." Mayor Suarez broke a giant purple seal on a giant envelope.

"So dramatic. I'm sure she already knows it's Bob and Premier," Charlotte said.

The mayor pulled the card from the envelope. "New Grant City Community Foundation."

People began to applaud.

Matt burned. "Bob stole our name and made a community foundation?"

"It's sinister," Charlotte raged. "He's trying to confuse our name in the community."

The mayor and governor looked around, unsure what to do.

"Is anyone here from the New Grant City Community Foundation?"

"Over here!"

Matt turned in the direction of Allan's voice.

"Over here!" With his height advantage, Allan stood out as he pointed in Matt and Charlotte's direction.

Mayor Juarez pointed at Matt from the podium. "Are you Matthew Wellington with New Grant City Community Foundation?"

Matt wasn't sure if he even answered. Nothing made sense in the moment. Allan guided him as he walked—or floated—to the platform.

The governor shook his hand and said, "Thank you for revitalizing Indiana by investing in this as a community center!"

Away from the mic, the mayor said, "I've heard of you and the work you are doing. I'm glad to finally meet you." She handed him a giant key and said into the mic, "Congratulations to Grant City and the New Grant City Community Foundation."

"Look at that camera!" someone ordered, but more than one camera snapped a picture.

Matt didn't know where to look or what to do. He just wanted to stay on his feet and not pass out.

The police ushered Matt down the stairs and onto street level. The FOX57 reporter stood next to him as the cameraman got into position. The red camera light came on.

"Mr. Wellington, congratulations on submitting the winning offer. How does it feel?"

Matt stared into the camera and said, "It feels like winning the lottery. It feels like I'm in a movie."

"Matthew Wellington!" Matt turned to the angry voice of Bob rushing towards him. "You are a—"

An agent from the governor's security detail tackled Bob. Another member had Bob's hands behind his back and cuffed within five seconds. "Stay on the ground!" someone shouted as the police rushed the governor and mayor off the stage.

Matt looked back to the camera, but it was focused on Bob raging on the sidewalk. Matt slipped away, found Charlotte, and hustled to the other side of Broadway as the crowd frantically scattered.

Charlotte grabbed the front of Matt's jacket and pulled him towards her. "What just happened? I mean, we were going to lunch, and then there's the governor! And there's a foundation! And Allan—where's Allan?"

"Right here!" Allan threw his arms around his brother and sister.

Charlotte punched him in the chest. "What just happened?"

"What just happened, Allan?" Matt grabbed his brother's shoulder and waved the key in the air. "Why do I have this?"

"Did Bob just threaten the Governor and get arrested?" Charlotte squealed. "Did you see them take him down?"

"He was threatening me." Matt looked at the scene with Bob and the police. "I should go over there and explain. But first...," he turned to Allan, "...explain what just happened."

"I resigned from my seat, and I said I wanted to help other Matts and invest in the community."

"And you started a foundation and purchased the community center?" Matt asked.

"I started a 501C3, and I had a large chunk I could put into it, but I wouldn't have the money to fix it up. Val at U-Up promised the funds to rehab it."

"Val? How did you contact her?"

"Through Reggie. And he also donated to it through his charity."

"He did?" Tears started down Charlotte's face.

Matt looked around for Reggie, who was standing down the street. Matt ran over to him. "Thank you!"

"Matt, I barely donated anything compared to U-Up."

"Why would they do that?"

"Matt, most people start a business with a purpose," Reggie said. "They want to help someone. And you and Charlotte and Allan are people who help people. When people realize that about you, they want to invest.

Besides, U-Up is looking to break into the Midwest region. A little engagement doesn't hurt, does it?"

"It doesn't."

"Being on TV with the governor and his Revitalize Indiana campaign is good for Engagement, too!"

"Yes. So you obviously knew about this?" Matt asked.

"I did. Allan contacted me after the last quarterly. We had a heart-to-heart about what he really wanted to do. Sounds like he's been a wise investor and has had money for NGC and for the community foundation. And he could do it because of the money he's making from NGC."

"Well, there's something else Allan and I have in common," Matt said.

"What's that?" Reggie asked.

Matt put his arm around Reggie's shoulder and faced the community center so Reggie wouldn't see his tears. "The best phone call we ever made was to you."

Reggie reciprocated, putting his arm around Matt. They stared at the theater in silence. Charlotte and Allan joined them.

They heard the rapid clicks of the digital camera from across the street. An event photographer with a long-range lens had shot at least a dozen pictures of them.

Charlotte laughed. "At least this time, Matt's in the middle of our family picture."

CHAPTER 33

The End

Matt and Reggie sipped a coffee from the back of the theater as they watched Charlotte open the community center's first event, a free one-day RISE course. Over 100 businesspeople registered.

"I don't think she needs me here to do this," Reggie said. "I think she could rejuvenate the local business owners on her own."

"She's good, Reggie, but she is still my sister. Besides, you're the star with all the social media followers and the best-selling book. That's why people are here."

"They will realize the value that Charlotte provides when she and I talk about systems and engagement this afternoon. And they will realize your value when we talk about resources and inspiration this morning."

"About our successes?"

"No. You're going to testify about how you would unclog toilets."

Matt laughed. "I think Charlotte is almost done. You're almost up."

They turned their attention to the stage.

Charlotte beamed in the bright lights of the attendees' attention. She was engaging, witty, and humorous.

"I never saw her coming," Matt said, shaking his head. "But it's a good thing she arrived."

Reggie grunted his approval.

"So, before I bring Reggie Singer up here," Charlotte announced, "I want you to remember that if you need anything today, you can stop me or my brothers or my arm-candy fiancée, Stan. Stand up, Stan!"

Stan obliged and sheepishly waved to the crowd. He looked like he felt naked without a cap.

"About twenty months ago, our company hit bottom. It was because Matt hit bottom, and he is the heart, soul, and inspiration of this team. He has always said a lot of crazy things when he is frantic. And that day, he said one of the craziest things: 'I'm going to get Reggie Singer to come coach us.' I had never heard of Reggie. I was learning this business on the fly. Reggie's coaching transformed us instantly. It hurts to have layer after layer peeled off. As a family, we had a lot of hard conversations. But because of Reggie's coaching, we have this community center, our booming business, and a TV show offer. But more important than that, I have a relationship with my brothers like I've never had before. So, before I start crying, I introduce to you Reggie Singer."

It was like Reggie flipped a switch and went into entertainer mode, running down to the front like he just got called to be on The Price is Right.

Charlotte joined Matt in the back, and they exited to the lobby. "I just had to get out of there for a moment to compose myself," Charlotte said, fanning her face.

"There you two are!" Allan approached with two identical packages in his hands. "I have a present for you two." He gave each of them one of the gifts. "Go ahead and open it. It's for your offices."

Matt ripped off the wrapping and discovered an unlabeled box. He opened it and pulled out a folded picture frame. Before he unfolded his, Charlotte said, "I love it, Allan! Thank you. It's going on my desk."

Matt opened the hinged two-picture frame. The picture on the left was taken by Allan on the day he announced that he was leaving. It was Charlotte hugging Matt after they had their heart-to-heart. Both of them were crying.

The second picture had been taken by the event photographer. It had the three of them and Reggie, arms around each other, stoically staring towards the theater.

"Why did you have to pick two pictures where I'm crying?" Matt asked.

"Because it's rare, like a bigfoot sighting!" Allan said.

"Guys, we have a long day ahead of us, so before we emotionally wear out, let's recharge by watching it again," Charlotte suggested.

Matt rubbed his hands together. "I haven't watched it in three weeks."

"I don't have to watch it. I was standing right there by the bottom of the steps," Allan said. "It's forever branded in my memory."

"Here it is. It's had over four million views in ten months now."

Charlotte held out her phone, and they watched the viral video clip that they could recite word-for-word.

The reporter congratulated Matt on submitting the winning offer and asked Matt how it felt. Matt stared into the camera and said, "It feels like winning the lottery. It feels like I'm in a movie." And that's when Bob appeared, charging Matt, and said, "Matthew Wellington! You are a—"

Charlotte paused the video. "I still wonder what he was going to say."

"I think he was going to curse," Matt said. "But this was a PG movie, so that security officer edited out the next words with the takedown."

"I think this video kept him out of jail," Allan offered. "He clearly is yelling your name and charging you."

"I love the way this video turned out," Charlotte said, "but Allan, wouldn't it be even better if Bob and Matt had grappled on the sidewalk?"

Allan laughed.

"No. It wouldn't have been better, Charlotte," Matt said.

Charlotte shrugged and continued playing the video. "The way Bob's face compresses and deforms against the cement is physically amazing."

"Is it still your desktop background?" Allan asked.

"No. I've matured a little since then," Charlotte said as she slid back the video progress bar and watched it again. "Ouch! His face."

Allan said, "I'd like to think that I could be as cool as the cameraperson. Some crazy screaming guy is rushing in her direction, and she had the composure to keep filming the crazy guy."

"Stay on the ground!" Charlotte said in her deepest voice, imitating the officer.

"Are they going to cover this viral video on our flippers show?" Matt asked. "That would be sweet if Bob was on one episode."

"Stay on the ground!" Charlotte repeated and giggled.

Plumber Stan burst through the theater doors. "Matt, Reggie wants you in there."

Matt deeply inhaled and exhaled. "It's showtime." He turned to his siblings and bit his lip to push through the emotions. "I couldn't have done this without the two of you. Did you ever think we could all realize our purpose like this?"

"No," Allan said. "But I believe that throughout all these years, you believed that we could."

Matt nodded. "Time to talk about how to RISE!"

THANK YOU FOR READING OUR BOOK!

Thank you so much for taking the time to read this book! We hope that this has helped to support you in developing your own business. To grow further, scan this QR code to take a free online business assessment to further your understanding of where you are struggling and direct you to success.

This will help your business RISE to 100%!

You can take our free online business assessment

by scanning the QR Code below:

We appreciate your interest in our book and value your feedback as it helps us improve future versions of this book. We would appreciate it if you could leave your invaluable review on Amazon.com with your feedback. Thank you!

www.ingramcontent.com/pod-product-compliance
Lightning Source LLC
Chambersburg PA
CBHW050257010526
44107CB00033B/1410/J